# Welcome to the World Heritage Ci[t]

There are places that somehow manage to get under your skin, even though you don't really know them all that well. Bruges is that kind of place. A warm and friendly place, a place made for people. A city whose history made it great, resulting in a well-deserved classification as a Unesco World Heritage site.

In this guide you will discover Bruges' different facets. There are five separate chapters.

In **chapter 1**, you will learn everything you need to know to prepare for your visit to Bruges. There is a list of the ten 'must-see' sights, a brief summary of the city's rich past, and a mass of practical information, including a clear explanation about how best to use the 'Bruges City Card'. This card will allow you to visit many of Bruges' most important sites of interest for free or at a significantly reduced price. This chapter also has plenty of useful eating-out suggestions for the lovers of fine food and drink and shopaholics can discover the best and most authentic retail addresses in town.

The three inspiring walking routes included in **chapter 2** will take you to all the most beautiful spots in town. The detailed map of the city – which you can simply fold out of the back cover of this guide – will make sure that you don't lose your way. The map also shows the licensed places to stay in Bruges, offering a range of accommodation options that runs from charming guest rooms and holiday homes right through to star-rated hotels.

C. ent options for getting around and gives an overview of the city's vibrant cultural life, with a summary of annual events and a full list of the city's museums, attractions and sites of interest, including all its historic, cultural and religious buildings. Bruges' beautiful squares and enchanting canals are the regular backdrop for topclass cultural events. And few cities have such a rich and diverse variety of museums, which contain gems ranging from the Flemish primitives and beautiful lace work to the finest modern art of today. Put simply, Bruges is always an experience – whether your interest is art, chocolate, diamonds or chips!

In Bruges you can dine at a different star-rated restaurant each day or perhaps you would prefer lunch at a trendy bistro before wandering through the winding cobbled streets of the city? Or maybe you just want to take in a pleasant pub or one of the many magnificent terraces with a view? These are the places, full of charm and character, which you can read about in **chapter 4**, Five 'new arrivals' to the city will also tell you about their favourite places in town.

You are staying a bit longer in the region? **Chapter 5** suggests a number of excursions to the other Flemish art towns, the Bruges Wetlands and Woodlands, the coast, the Westhoek, the Meetjesland (Creek Country) and the Flemish Ardennes. The choice is yours!

Begijnhofbrug

# Discover
# **Bruges**

# The highlights of Bruges
## The 10 classic places
## that no one should miss!

### Rozenhoedkaai,
### a living picture postcard

The Rozenhoedkaai links the Belfry to the city's network of canals ('reien'). So perhaps it was inevitable that the quay should become one of the most photogenic locations in all of Bruges. In fact, this spot is so special that it is almost impossible not to take a photograph: a living postcard that you can be a part of!

### A quiet moment in the Beguinage

Some places are just too pretty for words. The Beguinage is one such a place. It really leaves you speechless. All you can do is wander around and admire its beauty. This walled oasis of religious calm, with its impressive courtyard garden, its wind-bent trees, its white painted gables and its limitless silence, will charm even the greatest cynic. All year round. *(Also see page 74)*

## Burg and City Hall: medieval opulence

The Burg is one of the city's most beautiful squares. For more than six centuries, Bruges has been governed from its 14th-century City Hall, one of the oldest and most venerable in the Low Countries. All this time this remarkable historic building has dominated this majestic square. Nowhere else will you be able to experience the city's wealth and affluence so strongly. *(Also see page 90)*

## The Flemish primitives: timeless beauty  25  38

In the 15th century – Bruges' golden century – the fine arts reached their highest form of expression. Famous names such as Jan van Eyck and Hans Memling came to live and work in the city. Today, you can still admire the magnificent paintings of these world-famous Flemish primitives, standing face to face with masterpieces that were created more than 500 years ago in the very heart of Bruges. *(Also see pages 81-82, 87)*

## Wandering through the old Hansa Quarter

From the 13th to the 15th century, Bruges was an important trading centre at the crossroads between the Hansa cities of Scandinavia, England and Germany

(known collectively in those days as the 'Easterners') and the most important commercial regions in France, Spain and Italy. The Spanish traders established themselves at Spaanse Loskaai (Spanish Unloading Quay), while the Easterners set up shops on the Oosterlingenplein (Easterners' Square). Places where you can still feel the atmosphere of days long gone by.

## 🚢 The Canals of Bruges: the city's arteries

Experience the city by following an age-old tradition. Cruising Bruges' canals – the remarkable city arteries – you will discover secret gardens, picturesque bridges and wonderfully beautiful views. Although it sounds incredible, Bruges' loveliest places ooze even more charm when you admire them travelling by boat.

## The Church of Our Lady: the centuries-old skyline of Bruges 15 34

The Church of Our Lady (Onze-Lieve-Vrouwekerk) is most remarkable for its 115,5 metre-high brick tower, a tribute to the skill of the city's medieval crafts-men and the second highest tower of its kind in the world. Inside the church you can wonder at the beauty of the *Madonna and Child*, a marble masterpiece sculpted by Michelangelo and guaranteed to leave no visitor unmoved.

*(Also see pages 84-85)*

## 🏛 Almshouses: charity frozen in stone

Almshouses formed tiny villages within the city's ramparts. That's how these medieval residential courts – which are still occupied – are best described. Centuries ago they were built out of mortar and charity. Today their picturesque gardens, white façades and glorious silence are the city's havens of peace par excellence.

*(Also see page 36)*

## Concert Hall or Culture with a capital C 16

This imposing and intriguing culture temple is a beacon of light and provides 't Zand, the square on which it stands, with a unique dynamic all on its own. Inside, there is no elaborate theatrical decoration, but a simple, almost minimalist, auditorium with a 'symphonic' arrangement of chairs. In short, the ideal circumstances in which to enjoy classical concerts, jazz, dance or theatre. *(More information on page 93)*

## Market Square – a must 10 04 27

If there is only one place you can visit in Bruges, this is it. The Market Square is the beating heart of the city. The colourful guild houses, the clatter of horses' hooves, the rattling of the carriages and the dominating presence of the Belfry all combine to create a setting of great beauty and charm, which is part medieval and part modern. And if you are feeling energetic, you can still climb the 366 steps of the 83-metre high belfry tower, which will reward you with a spectacular panorama over the city and its surrounding hinterland. The Market is also the home of Historium, a top attraction that takes you back to the golden days of Bruges in the Middle Ages. The balcony on the first floor has a fine view of the square, with its statue of Jan Breydel and Pieter de Coninck, two of the city's most important historical figures. *(For more information about the Belfry see also pages 74-75 and about Historium see page 82)*

# History in a nutshell

Water played a crucial role in the birth and development of Bruges. It was at this place that a number of streams converged to form the River Reie, which then flowed northwards towards the coastal plain. Through a series of tidal creeks, the river eventually reached the sea. Little wonder, then, that even as far back as Roman times there was already considerable seafaring activity in this region. This has been proven by the discovery of the remains of two seagoing ships from this period, dating from the second half of the 3$^{rd}$ century or the first half of the 4$^{th}$ century. Even so, it would be another five centuries before the name 'Bruges' first began to appear – the word being a derivative of the old-German word 'brugj', which means 'mooring place'.

Its growing importance also resulted in it becoming the main fortified residence of the counts of Flanders, so that from the 11th century onwards the city was not only a prosperous trading metropolis, but also a seat of considerable political power.

## Taking off

When the city's direct link with the sea was in danger of silting-up in the 12th century, Bruges went through a period of anxiety. Fortunately, the new waterway of the Zwin brought relief. As a result, Bruges was able to call itself the most important trade centre of Northwest Europe in the following century. The world's first stock exchange began business. Its financial exchanges took place on a square in front of the premises that belonged to Van der Beurse, a Bruges merchant family. In spite of the typical medieval maladies, from epidemics to political unrest and social inequality, the citizens of Bruges prospered, and soon the city developed a magnet-like radiation. Around 1340 the inner city numbered no fewer than 35.000 inhabitants.

## Golden Age

Success continually increased. In the 15th century – Bruges' Golden Age – things improved further when the Royal House of Burgundy took up residence in the city. New luxury goods were produced and sold in abundance, and famous painters such as Jan van Eyck and Hans Memling – the great Flemish primitives – found their creative niche here.

The fine arts flourished, and besides a substantial number of fine churches and unique merchant houses, a monumental town hall was also erected. Bruges' success seemed imperishable.

## Decline

The death of the popular Mary of Burgundy in 1482 marked a sudden change of fortune. The relationship between the citizens of Bruges and their lord, the widower Maximilian, turned sour. The Burgundian court left the city, with the international traders following in its wake. Long centuries of wars and changes of political power took their toll. By the middle of the 19th century Bruges had become an impoverished city. Remarkably enough, a novel was partly responsible for giving a boost to the revival of the city.

## Revival

With great care, Bruges took its first steps into tourism. In *Bruges la Morte* (1892), Georges Rodenbach aptly describes Bruges as a somewhat sleepy, yet extremely mysterious place. Soon Bruges' magnificent patrimony was rediscovered and her mysterious intimacy turned out to be her greatest asset. Building on this enthusiasm, the city was provided with a new seaport, which was called Zeebrugge. The pulling power of Bruges proved to be a great success and UNESCO added the medieval city centre to its World Heritage list. The rest is history.

## From early settlement to international trade centre
### (...-1200)

**851** Earliest record of the city

**863** Baldwin I takes up residence at Burg

**1127** Charles the Good, Count of Flanders, is murdered in the Church of Saint Donatian; first town rampart; first Bruges city charter

**1134** Creation of the Zwin – evolving from the Sincfal marshes – that links Damme with the sea

## Bruges' Golden Age
### (1369-1500)

**1369** Margaret of Dampierre marries Philip the Bold, Duke of Burgundy. Beginning of the Burgundian period

**1384** Margaret succeeds her father Louis of Male

**1430** Marriage of Duke Philip the Good with Isabella of Portugal; establishment of the Order of the Golden Fleece

**1436** Jan van Eyck paints the panel *Madonna with Canon Joris van der Paele*

**1482** Mary of Burgundy dies as a result of a fall with her horse

**1488** Maximilian of Austria is locked up in Craenenburg House on Markt for a few weeks

**851** **1200** **1300** **1500**

## Bruges as the economic capital of Northwest Europe
### (1200-1400)

**1245** Foundation of the Beguinage

**1280** Reconstruction in stone of the Belfry after the destruction of its wooden predecessor

**1297** Second town rampart

**1302** Bruges Matins and Battle of the Golden Spurs

**1304** First Procession of the Holy Blood

**1376-1420** Construction of the City Hall

## The city gets her second wind
### (1500-1578)

**1506** The cloth merchant Jan Mouscron acquires Michelangelo's *Madonna and Child*

**1528** Lancelot Blondeel designs the mantelpiece of the Liberty of Bruges

**1548** Birth of the scientist Simon Stevin

**1562** Marcus Gerards engraves the first printed town map of Bruges

**1578** Bruges joins the rebellion against the Spanish king

## An impoverished town in a pauperised Flanders (1584-1885)

**1584** Bruges becomes reconciled with the Spanish king

**1604** The Zwin is closed off

**1713-1795** Austrian period

**1717** Foundation of the Academy of Fine Arts, which formed the basis for the collection of the Groeninge Museum.

**1795-1814** French period

**1799** Demolition of Saint Donatian's Cathedral and renovation of Burg

**1815-1830** United Kingdom of the Netherlands

**1830** Independence of Belgium; birth of the poet Guido Gezelle

**1838** First railway station

## The new city (1971-...)

**1971** Amalgamation Law incorporates former suburbs

**1985** King Baudouin opens new sea lock at Zeebrugge

**2000** Historic city centre is given World Heritage status; Euro 2000 (European Football Championship)

**2002** Cultural Capital of Europe

**2008** *In Bruges* is released worldwide in cinemas

**2010** The Procession of the Holy Blood is granted Intangible Cultural Heritage status by UNESCO

**1600**  **1700**  **1800**  **1900**  **2000**

## Provincial town with revived ambitions (1885-1970)

**1887** Unveiling of the statue of Jan Breydel and Pieter de Coninck (Markt)

**1892** Publication of *Bruges la Morte* by Georges Rodenbach

**1896** Start of the construction of the seaport

**1897** Dutch becomes the official language

**1902** First important exhibition of the Flemish primitives

**1914-1918** The Great War; Bruges is a German naval base

**1940-1945** The historic city centre survives Second World War almost unscathed

**1958** First Pageant of the Golden Tree

# Practical information

## Brugge City Card

Get to know the city in all its many facets and save money at the same time! With the **Brugge City Card** you can visit 27 museums and attractions in Bruges for free. The trips on the canals or 'reien' (sailings only guaranteed during the period 1/3 to 15/11) are also free of charge. In addition, the Bruges City Card also guarantees a discount of at least 25% on a three-day pass for De Lijn (bus service), on numerous concerts, dance and theatre productions, on rental bikes, on underground parking and on various museums, attractions and other places of interest in the area around Bruges.

### HOW DOES IT WORK?

You choose the validity period of your **Brugge City Card**: **48 hours** or **72 hours**. In the chapters *Exploring Bruges, Finding your way around Bruges* and *Excursions from Bruges* you will find a detailed overview of all the guided tours, attractions, museums and places of interest in and around the city. If you see a 🎫, you will get in **for free** with your Bruges City Card; a 🎫 means that you will **receive at least a 25% discount** on the individual price. What's more, in the free monthly event calendar you can find a helpful list of all the events that you can visit at reduced costs using your Bruges City Card. When you use your Bruges City Card for the first time, it is automatically activated. Once the validity period has elapsed, the card automatically stops working. You can only visit each attraction once. Bear in mind that many of the city's museums are closed on Monday.

### WHAT DOES IT COST?

(48h) **€ 46.00**   (72h) **€ 49.00**

### HOW TO ORDER?

Just drop by the tourist offices on the ℹ️ Markt (Market Square - Historium), 't Zand (Zand Square - Concert Hall) or the Stationsplein (Station Square - station) or order your Bruges City Card online via www.bruggecitycard.be

# Bicycle rental points

### Bauhaus Bike Rental
**LOCATION >** Langestraat 145
**PRICE >** 3 hours: € 6.00; full day: € 9.00
(Brugge City Card: € 6.00)
**OPENING TIMES >** Daily, 8.00 a.m.-8.00
p.m. (bikes must be returned by 8.00 p.m.)
**INFORMATION >** Tel. +32 (0)50 34 10 93,
www.bauhaus.be/services/bike-rental

### B-Bike Concertgebouw
**LOCATION >** 't Zand
**PRICE >** 1 hour: € 4.00; 4 hours: € 8.00; full
day: € 12.00 (Brugge City Card: € 9.00)
**OPENING TIMES >** During the period 1/4 to
15/10: daily, 10.00 a.m.-7.00 p.m.; during
the period 16/10 to 31/3: weekends only
10.00 a.m.-12.00 a.m. and 1.00 p.m.-
7.00 p.m.
**INFO >** Tel. +32 (0)479 97 12 80,
info@b-bike.be

### Bruges Bike Rental
**LOCATION >** Niklaas Desparsstraat 17
**PRICE >** 1 hour: € 3.50; 2 hours: € 5.00;
4 hours: € 7.00; full day: € 10.00; students
(on display of a valid student card): € 8.00.
Price tandem 1 hour: € 8.00; 2 hours:
€ 12.00; 4 hours: € 15.00; full day: € 20.00;
students (on display of a valid student
card): € 17.00
**OPENING TIMES >** During the period 1/2 to
28/12: daily: 10.00 a.m.-8.00 p.m.
**INFO >** Tel. +32 (0)50 61 61 08,
www.brugesbikerental.be

### De Ketting
**LOCATION >** Gentpoortstraat 23
**PRICE >** € 6.00/day. Price electric bike:
€ 20,00/day
**OPENING TIMES >** During the period 1/4
to 1/10: Monday to Saturday, 10.00 a.m.-
6.30 p.m., Sunday, 10.30 a.m.-6.30 p.m.;
during the period 2/10 to 31/3: Monday to
Saturday, 10.00 a.m.-6.30 p.m.
**INFO >** Tel. +32 (0)50 34 41 96,
www.deketting.be

### Electric Scooters
Hire of electric bikes.
**LOCATION >** Gentpoortstraat 55 and 62
**PRICE >** 2 hours: € 10.00; 4 hours: € 18.00
and 8 hours: € 30.00
**OPENING TIMES >** During the period 1/4
to 30/09: Tuesday to Sunday, 10.00 a.m.-6.00
p.m.; during the period 1/10 to 31/3: Tuesday
to Saturday, 1.00 p.m.-6.00 p.m. (from 10.00
a.m. on appointment and with a reservation)
**EXTRA >** Electric scooters *(See page 71)*
**INFO >** Tel. +32 (0)474 09 19 18,
info@electric-scooters.be,
www.electric-scooters.be

### Eric Popelier
**LOCATION >** Mariastraat 26
**PRICE >** 1 hour: € 4.00; 4 hours: € 8.00; full
day: € 12.00 (Brugge City Card: € 9.00).
Price electric bike 1 hour: € 10.00; 4 hours:
€ 17.00; full day: € 30.00. Price tandem
1 hour: € 10.00; 4 hours: € 17.00; full day:
€ 25.00 (Brugge City Card: € 18,75); price
reduction for students
**OPENING TIMES >** During the period 1/3 to
31/10: daily, 10.00 a.m.-7.00 p.m.; during
the period 1/11 to 28/2: Tuesday to Saturday,
10.00 a.m.-6.00 p.m.
**INFO >** Tel. +32 (0)50 34 32 62,
www.fietsenpopelier.be

### Fietspunt Station
**LOCATION >** Hendrik Brugmansstraat 3
(Stationsplein, Railway station Square)
**PRICE >** City bike, 1 hour: € 4.00; 4 hours:
€ 8.00; full day: € 12.00 (Brugge City Card:
€ 9.00). Electric bike, full day: € 30.00

**OPENING TIMES >** Monday to Friday,
7.00 a.m-7.30 p.m.; during the period
1/4 to 30/11: also during weekends and
on holidays, 9.00 a.m.-9.30 p.m.
**ADDITIONAL CLOSING DATES >** 1/1 and 2/1
**INFO >** Tel. +32 (0)50 39 68 26
fietspunt.brugge@groepintro.be

**Koffieboontje**
**LOCATION >** Hallestraat 4
**PRICE >** 1 hour: € 4.00; 4 hours: € 8.00; full
day: € 12.00 (Brugge City Card: € 9.00);
students (on display of a valid student
card): € 9.00. Price tandem 1 hour: € 10.00;
4 hours: € 18.00; full day: € 25.00
**OPENING TIMES >** Daily, 9.00 a.m.-
10.00 p.m.
**INFO >** Tel. +32 (0)50 33 80 27,
www.bikerentalkoffieboontje.be

**Snuffel Backpacker Hostel**
**LOCATION >** Ezelstraat 47-49
(from May 1st 2015: Ezelstraat 42)
**PRICE >** Full day: € 8.00 (Brugge City Card:
€ 6.00)
**OPENING TIMES >** Daily, 8.00 a.m.-8.00 p.m.
**INFO >** Tel. +32 (0)50 33 31 33,
www.snuffel.be

Most of the bicycle rental points ask for the
payment of a guarantee.

## Campers

The Kanaaleiland (Canal Island) at the
Bargeweg offers excellent hard standing
for 57 campers all year round. Once your
camper is parked, you are just a five-
minute walk from the city centre (via the
Beguinage). The parking area is open
for new arrivals until 10.00 p.m. It is not
possible to make prior reservations.
**PRICE >** During the period 1/4 to 30/9:
€ 22.50/day; during the period 1/10 to 31/3:
€ 15.00/day. Free electricity; it is also possible to stock up with clean water (€ 0.50) and
dispose of dirty water.

## Church services

**01** **Basiliek van het Heilig Bloed
(Basilica of the Holy Blood)**
Daily (except Thursday): 11.00 a.m.

**02** **Begijnhofkerk (Beguinage)**
Monday to Saturday: 7.15 a.m.,
Sunday: 9.30 a.m.

**12** **English Church**
('t Keerske / Saint Peter's Chapel)
English language Anglican service,
Sunday: 6.00 p.m.

**09** **Jezuïetenhuis (Jesuits)**
Monday to Friday: 12.00 p.m.,
Saturday: 5.00 p.m., Sunday: 11.30 a.m.

**10** **Kapucijnenkerk (Capuchins)**
Monday to Friday: 8.00 a.m.,
Saturday: 6.00 p.m., Sunday: 10.00 a.m.

**11** **Karmelietenkerk (Carmelites)**
Monday-Friday 7.00 a.m.,
Saturday: 6.00 p.m., Sunday: 10.00 a.m.

**15** **Onze-Lieve-Vrouwekerk
(Church of Our Lady)**
Saturday: 5.30 p.m., Sunday: 11.00 a.m.

**16** **Onze-Lieve-Vrouw-ter-Potteriekerk
(Our Lady of the Pottery)**
Monday to Friday: 6.45 a.m.,
Sunday: 7.00 a.m. and 9.30 a.m.

**17** **Onze-Lieve-Vrouw-van-
Blindekenskapel (Our Lady of the Blind)**
First Saturday of the month: 6.00 p.m.

**18** **Orthodoxe Kerk HH. Konstantijn
& Helena (Orthodox Church Saints
Constantin & Helen)**
Saturday: 6.00 p.m., Sunday: 9.00 a.m.

**19** **Sint-Annakerk (Saint Anne)**
Sunday: 10.00 a.m.

**Sint-Gilliskerk (Saint Giles)**
Sunday: 7.00 p.m.

 **Sint-Jakobskerk (Saint James)**
Saturday: 6.30 p.m.

 **Sint-Salvatorskathedraal
(Saint Saviour)**
Monday to Friday: 6.00 p.m.,
Saturday: 4.00 p.m., Sunday: 10.30 a.m.

 **Verenigde Protestantse Kerk
(United Protestant Church)**
('t Keerske / Saint Peter's Chapel)
Sunday: 10.00 a.m.

 **Vrije Evangelische Kerk
(Free Evangelical Church)**
Sunday: 10.00 a.m.

## Cinemas

» All films are shown in their original
language.

 **Cinema Liberty**
Kuipersstraat 23, www.cinema-liberty.be

 **Cinema Lumière**
Sint-Jakobsstraat 36, www.lumierecinema.be

 **Kinepolis Brugge**
Koning Albert I-laan 200, Sint-Michiels,
www.kinepolis.com | bus: no. 27, stop:
Kinepolis

## Climate

Bruges enjoys a mild, maritime climate. The
summers are warm without being hot and
the winters are cold without being freezing.
During spring and autumn the temperatures
are also pleasant and there is moderate
rainfall throughout the year, with the heavi-
est concentrations in autumn and winter. So
remember to bring your umbrella!

## Emergencies
### ▶ European emergency number
» tel. 112. This general number is used in
all countries of the European Union to contact the emergency services: police, fire
brigade or medical assistance. The number operates 24 hours a day, 7 days a week.

### ▶ Medical help
» **Doctors, pharmacists, dentists
and nursing officers on duty**
tel. 1733
» **S.O.S. Emergency Service**
tel. 100
» **Hospitals**
A.Z. St.-Jan > tel. +32 (0)50 45 21 11
A.Z. St.-Lucas > tel. +32 (0)50 36 91 11
St.-Franciscus Xaveriuskliniek >
tel. +32 (0)50 47 04 70
» **Poisons Advice Centre**
tel. +32 (0)70 245 245

### ▶ Police
» **General telephone number**
tel. +32 (0)50 44 88 44
» **Emergency police assistance**    tel. 101
» **Working hours**
Monday to Saturday: 8.00 a.m.- 6.00 p.m.
you can contact the central police services
at Kartuizerinnenstraat 4 | City map: E9
» **After working hours**
There is a 24/24 permanence at the police
station at the Lodewijk Coiseaukaai 3 |
City map: F1

## Formalities
» **Identity**
An identity card or valid passport is neces-
sary. Citizens of the European Union do not
require an entrance visa. If you arrive in
Belgium from outside the European Union,
you must first pass through customs.
There are no border controls once inside
the European Union.
» **Health**
Citizens of the European Union can use their
own national health insurance card/docu-

ment to obtain free medical treatment in Belgium. You can obtain this card from your own national health service. Please note, however, that every member of the family must have his/her own card/document.

## Getting there
### ▶ By car/coach/ferry
From the UK you travel to Bruges by ferry or by Eurotunnel:

» **Hull (UK) – Zeebrugge (B)** with P&O Ferries. (crossing: 13h30). Take the N31 from Zeebrugge to Bruges. Estimated distance Zeebrugge – Bruges is 17km or 11 miles (30min driving).

» **Dover (UK) – Dunkerque (F)** with DFDS Seaways (crossing: 1h45). Take the motorway E40 to Bruges. Estimated distance Dunkerque – Bruges is 76km or 47 miles (1h driving).

» **Dover (UK) – Calais (F)** with P&O Ferries or DFDS Seaways (crossing: 1h30). Estimated distance Calais – Bruges is 120km or 75 miles (1h30 driving).

» **Folkestone (UK) – Calais (F)** via Eurotunnel (35min). Estimated distance Calais – Bruges is 120km or 75 miles (1h30 driving).

**A 30 kph zone is in force throughout the entire city centre. This means that you are forbidden at all times to drive faster than 30 kilometres per hour.**
Parking is for an unlimited time and is most advantageous in one of the two city centre car parks: at the station (€ 0.70/hour and € 3.50/24 hours) or under the Zand Square (€ 1.20/hour and € 8.70/24 hours).
*(For more information, see 'Parking')*

### ▶ By train
» **National**
The station at Brussel-Zuid (Brussels South) is the Belgian hub for international rail traffic. Numerous high speed trains arrive in Brussel-Zuid daily, coming from Paris (Thalys and TGV), Lille (Eurostar and TGV), London (Eurostar), Amsterdam (Thalys) and Cologne (Thalys and ICE). Every hour two trains for Ostend or Knokke/Blankenberge (stopping at Bruges) depart from Brussel-Zuid. The travelling time between Brussel-Zuid and Bruges is approximately 1 hour.

### ▶ By plane
» **Via Brussels Airport**
Each day, the national airport at Zaventem welcomes flights from more than 200 cities in 66 countries. It is easy to travel from Brussels

### ▶ How to get to Bruges?

| departure | via | km | mls | time train ◷ | time bus ◷ | time boat ◷ | make a reservation |
|---|---|---|---|---|---|---|---|
| Amsterdam | Brussels-South/-Midi | 253 | 157 | 03:06 | - | - | www.b-europe.com |
| Brussels Airport | - | 110 | 68 | 01:29 | - | - | www.belgianrail.be |
| Brussels South Charleroi Airport | - | 148 | 91 | - | 02:10 | - | www.flibco.com |
| Dover | Dunkerque | - | - | - | - | 02:00 | www.dfds.com |
| Dover | Calais | - | - | - | - | 01:30 | www.poferries.com, www.dfds.com & www.myferrylink.com |
| Hull | Zeebrugge | - | - | - | - | 1 night | www.poferries.com |
| Lille Flandres | Kortrijk | 75 | 47 | 01:47 | - | - | www.b-europe.com |
| London St Pancras | Brussels-South/-Midi | - | - | 03:24 | - | - | www.eurostar.com |

national airport to Bruges by train. On weekdays, there is a direct hourly service. You can also take the Brussels Airport Express (four trains every hour) to Brussel-Noord (Brussels-North), Brussel-Centraal (Brussels-Central) or Brussel-Zuid (Brussels-South). Every hour, two trains leave from these stations for Ostend or Knokke/Blankenberge, stopping in Bruges. For more information on timetables and rates, please refer to the website of the NMBS (Belgian National Railways): www.b-rail.be. Provided you have reserved in advance, taxi rides to and from Brussels national airport are available from Bruges taxi services at a fixed rate of € 200 (price adjustments are possible throughout the year).

### » Via Brussels South Charleroi Airport

This popular regional airport receives multiple low cost flights every day from various cities and regions in Europe. The Flibco.com bus company (www.flibco.com) provides a direct shuttle bus service to and from the station in Bruges, with a frequency of 9 trips per day (there and back). The shuttle bus is comfortable, fast and cheap. If you book in advance (online), it is even cheaper. The Bruges taxi services drive to and from Brussels South Charleroi Airport at a fixed rate of € 250 (price adjustments throughout the year are possible). Reservations must be made in advance.

### » In Bruges

From the station in Bruges, you can travel to your overnight accommodation address by bus (every 5 minutes: *see the section 'Public transport'*) or by taxi (*see 'Taxis'*).

## Good to know

With its wide shopping streets, inviting terraces, trendy eating houses and stylish hotels, Bruges is a paradise for shoppers. But don't let your shopping pleasure be ruined by pickpockets. Always keep your **wallet/purse** in a closed inside pocket, and not in an open handbag or rucksack. A golden tip for ladies: always close your handbag and wear it with the fastener against your body. Remember – thieves like shopping too!

Bruges is a lively, fun-loving city, with great nightlife. There are plenty of places where you can amuse yourself until the early hours of the morning. Please bear in mind that it is forbidden to sell **strong drink** (15% or more) to people under 18 years of age. For people under 16 years of age, this prohibition also applies to beer and wine (all drinks with an alcoholic content in excess of 0.5%). Visiting Bruges means endless hours of fun, but please allow the visitors who come after you to enjoy their fun in a **clean** and **tidy** city: so always put your rubbish in a rubbish bin.

##  Info on the go

In Bruges, 99 taxi drivers, coachmen and boatmen can call themselves 'touristic ambassadors of the city' following their successful completion of the course 'info on the go', which is all about customer-friendliness and an excellent knowledge of the city and its sights. These ambassadors can be identified by the 'info on the go' logo.

## Lockers

**Station (railway station)**
Stationsplein | City map: C12

 Historium
Markt 1

## Market days

### » Monday
8.00 a.m.-1.30 p.m. | Onder de Toren - Lissewege | miscellaneous
### » Wednesday
8.00 a.m.-1.30 p.m. | Markt | food and flowers
### » Friday
8.00 a.m.-1.30 a.m. | Market Square - Zeebrugge | miscellaneous

>> **Saturday**

8.00 a.m.-1.30 p.m. | 't Zand and Beursplein | miscellaneous

>> **Sunday**

7.00 a.m.-2.00 p.m. | Veemarkt, Sint-Michiels | miscellaneous

>> **Tuesday to Saturday**

8.00 a.m.-1.30 p.m. | Vismarkt | fish

>> **Daily**

8.00 a.m.-7.00 p.m. | Vismarkt | artisanal products

>> **Saturday, Sunday, public holidays and bridge days in the period 15/3 to 15/11 + also on Friday in the period June to September**

10.00 a.m.-6.00 p.m. | Dijver | antique, bric-à-brac and crafts

## Money

Most of the banks in Bruges are open from 9.00 a.m. to 12.30 p.m. and from 2.00 p.m. to 4.30 p.m. Many branch offices are also open on Saturday morning, but on Sunday they are all closed. There are cash points in several shopping streets, on 't Zand, the Simon Stevinplein, the Stationsplein (Railway station Square) and on the Bargeplein (Barge Market). You can easily withdraw money from cash machines with Visa, Eurocard or MasterCard. Currency can be exchanged in every bank or in an exchange office. In the event of the loss or theft of your bank or credit card, it is best to immediately block the card by calling Card Stop on tel. 070 344 344 (24 hours a day).

>> **Goffin Change**

Steenstraat 2 | City map: E8

>> **Pillen R.W.J.**

Rozenhoedkaai 2 | City map: F8
Vlamingstraat 18 | City map: E7

>> **New Best Money Change**

Sint-Amandsstraat 5 | City map: E8

## Opening hours

Most shops open their doors at 10.00 a.m. and close at 6.00 p.m. or 6.30 p.m. from Monday to Saturday. Some shops are also open on Sunday afternoon. Cafés and restaurants have no (fixed) closing hour. Sometimes they will remain open until the early hours of the morning and other days they will close earlier: it all depends on the number of customers.

## Parking

Bruges is a compact city. Most places of interest are within walking distance of your accommodation. In order to keep the historic city centre attractive and accessible, above-ground parking in the city centre is limited to a maximum of 4 hours in the Blue Zone and to 2 hours in the Pay&Display Zones. You can easily park your car in one of the underground car parks, which is usually less expensive. The most inexpensive and largest car parks are in front of the railway station (City map D13 - € 3.50/24 hours) or under 't Zand (€ 8,70/24 hours). Both are situated within walking distance of the city centre, but you can also use the bus transfer with De Lijn to and from the city centre (included in your parking fee for 4 passengers). Check the website www.interparking.com for any updates. The Park and Ride areas are situated right outside of the city centre. Here you can park your car for free and for a longer duration. The city centre is a stone's throw away on foot or by bus. If you are staying in Bruges, ask about parking spots near your place of accommodation in advance. Holders of a Bruges City Card (www.bruggecitycard.be) receive a 25% discount at the underground car parks operated by Interparking.

▶ **Parking Centrum-Station**
**CAPACITY >** 1500
**OPENING TIMES >** Daily, 24 hours a day
**PRICE >** Maximum € 3.50/24hrs (Brugge City Card: a discount of at least 25 %) | hourly rate: € 0.70

▶ **Parking Centrum-Zand**
**CAPACITY >** 1400
**OPENING TIMES >** Daily, 24 hours a day

**PRICE >** Maximum € 8.70/24hrs (Brugge City Card: a discount of at least 25 %) | hourly rate: € 1.20; from the second hour you pay per quarter. Check the website www.interparking.com for any updates.

## Post offices

» **BPost Markt**
Markt 5 | City map: E8
» **BPost Beursplein**
Sint-Maartensbilk 14 | City map: B10
*For posting letters, cards, etc. and for the purchase of stamps you can go to one of the postal points or stamp shops that you will find in various shopping streets throughout the city.*

## Public holidays

Belgium has quite a lot of public holidays. On these holidays most companies, shops, offices and public services are closed.
» 1 January (New Year's Day)
» 5 April (Easter Sunday) and 6 April (Easter Monday)
» 1 May (Labour Day)
» 14 May (Ascension Day)
» 24 May (Whit Sunday) and 25 May (Whit Monday)
» 11 July (Flemish regional holiday)
» 21 July (Belgian national holiday)
» 15 August (Assumption of Mary)
» 1 November (All Saints' Day)
» 11 November (Armistice Day)
» 25 December (Christmas)
» 26 December (Boxing Day)

## Public transport

▶ **Bus**
You can use public transport during your stay. De Lijn connects the railway station and the centre by bus every five minutes. From the Bargeplein (City map: E13), close to the spot where the tourist buses stop, there are also frequent services to the station and the city centre. The most important of the city's bus stops are marked with a bus pictogram

on the foldout map at the back of this guide. A bus ticket (single trip) is valid for 1 hour. You can buy a ticket for € 1.30 at a 'De Lijn' (bus service) ticket counter or for € 2.00 on the bus. When you purchase a Bruges City Card (www.bruggecitycard.be), you can also buy a three-day pass for De Lijn for € 6.00. This pass is valid on all buses and trams in Flanders. Like the Bruges City Card, you can buy the three-day pass at the 🛈 Tourist office near the station.

▶ **Tickets**
» **Advanced booking offices**
De Lijnwinkel, Stationsplein (railway station)
🛈 Tourist office Markt (Historium)
🛈 Tourist office 't Zand (Concertgebouw)
Various city centre bookshops, newsagents and department stores
» **Vending machines De Lijn**
De Lijnwinkel, Stationsplein (railway station)
Bus stop 't Zand
» **Information** www.delijn.be

## Smoking

In Belgium there is a general ban on smoking in cafés, restaurants, the public areas in hotels (lobby, bar, corridors, etc.) and in all public buildings (train stations, airports, etc.). Those unable to kick the habit will usually find an ashtray just outside (often under shelter).

## Swimming pools

**11 Interbad**
**INFO >** Veltemweg 35, Sint-Kruis, tel. +32 (0)50 35 07 77, interbad@skynet.be, www.interbad.be; bus: no. 10 or no. 58, stop: Watertoren

**12 Jan Guilini**
**INFO >** Keizer Karelstraat 41, tel. +32 (0)50 31 35 54, sportdienst@brugge.be, www.brugge.be/sport; bus: no. 9, stop: Visartpark

**13** **S&R Olympia**

INFO > This Olympic-sized pool (10 lanes of 50 metres) and its subtropical swimming pool annex opens its doors from the end of May. Doornstraat 110, Sint-Andries, Olympia@sr-olympia.be, www.sr-olympia.be; bus: no. 25, stop: Jan Breydel or no. 5, stop: Lange Molen.

All information about opening times is available at the **ℹ** Tourist office Markt (Historium), 't Zand (Concertgebouw) or Stationsplein (Station, railway station).

## Taxis

Whoever takes a taxi in Bruges with the logo 'info on the go' can enjoy all the benefits of a Certified Info Driver. As 'ambassadors' for Bruges, these taxi-drivers will tell you with great enthusiasm all about their city and will help to put you in just the right mood for your city visit.

TAXI STANDS > Markt and Stationsplein

TARIFFS > The local taxi companies all use the same fixed rate tariffs (adjustments are possible throughout the year):

  Bruges <> Brussels Airport: € 200.00
  Bruges <> Brussels South Charleroi Airport: € 250.00
  Bruges <> Aéroport de Lille: € 140.00

Please note: when you want to take a taxi from one of the airports to Bruges, you can only benefit from the above tariffs if you book the taxi in advance.

## Telephoning

If you want to phone someone in Bruges from abroad, you must first dial the country code (00)32, followed by the zone code 50, and then number of the person you want. To phone Bruges from inside Belgium, you dial 050 plus the number of the person.

## Toilets

There are a number of public toilets in Bruges (see the fold-out plan at the back of the guide). Some are accessible for wheelchair users, others have baby-changing areas. You will also find (free) toilets in some of the larger department stores or at the station. When local people need the toilet, they often pop into a cafe or pub to order something small so that they can use the facilities there.

## **ℹ** Tourist offices

There are three tourist information offices in Bruges: one in the Historium (Market Square), one in the Concertgebouw (Concert Hall) and a third in the railway station.

» **Tourist office Markt (Historium)**
Markt 1
Daily: 10.00 a.m.-5.00 p.m.
» **Tourist office 't Zand (Concertgebouw)**
't Zand
Monday to Saturday: 10.00 a.m.-5.00 p.m.
Sunday and public holidays: 10.00 a.m.-2.00 p.m.
» **Tourist office Stationsplein (Station, railway station)**
Stationsplein
Monday to Friday: 10.00 a.m.-5.00 p.m.
Saturday and Sunday: 10.00 a.m.-2.00 p.m.

All tourist offices are closed on Christmas Day and New Year's Day. For more information: tel. +32 (0)50 44 46 46, toerisme@brugge.be, www.visitbruges.be

## Travelling season

Although most visitors come to the city in the spring and summer months, Bruges has something to offer all year round. The misty months of autumn and winter are ideal for atmospheric strolls along the canals and the cobbled streets, before ending up in a cosy restaurant or cheerful pub. The 'cold' months are also perfect for undisturbed visits to the city's many museums and sites of interest, before again finishing up in one of those same restaurants or pubs! What's more, in January, February and March you can get great discounts on many accommodation outlets in Bruges.

# Bruges for bon-vivants

Bruges is a paradise for food connoisseurs. Its culinary delights range from Michelin-star establishments of international quality and reputation, through stylish local bistros and brasseries, to traditional Italian or Asian specialty restaurants.

## Award winning restaurants

Bruges is one of the gastronomic centres of Europe and boasts an impressive number of star-rated restaurants. Whether you swear by fish or prefer meat; whether you love beer in your dishes or would rather have a wine-based sauce; whether you are a fan of exotic culinary delights or a devotee of authentic, local cooking, the superior kitchens in Bruges have so much to offer that everyone will be able to discover recipe to his or her taste.

» **De Karmeliet**  Langestraat 19, 8000 Brugge, tel. +32 (0)50 33 82 59, www.dekarmeliet.be (3 Michelin-stars, 17/20 graded by GaultMillau)
» **De Jonkman**  Maalse Steenweg 438, 8310 Sint-Kruis, tel. +32 (0)50 36 07 67, www.dejonkman.be (2 Michelin-stars, 18/20 graded by GaultMillau)
» **Den Gouden Harynck**  Groeninge 25, 8000 Brugge, tel. +32 (0)50 33 76 37, www.goudenharynck.be (1 Michelin-star, 17/20 graded by GaultMillau)

- » **Auberge De Herborist**   De Watermolen 15, 8200 Sint-Andries, tel. +32 (0)50 38 76 00, www.aubergedeherborist.be (1 Michelin-star, 16/20 graded by GaultMillau)
- » **A'Qi**   Gistelse Steenweg 686, 8200 Sint-Andries, tel. +32 (0)50 30 05 99, www.restaurantaqui.be (1 Michelin-star, 16/20 graded by GaultMillau)
- » **Sans Cravate**   Langestraat 159, 8000 Brugge, tel. +32 (0)50 67 83 10, www.sanscravate.be (1 Michelin-star, 16/20 graded by GaultMillau)
- » **Zeno**   Vlamingstraat 53, 8000 Brugge, tel. +32 (0)50 68 09 93, www.restaurantzeno.be (16/20 graded by GaultMillau)
- » **Goffin**   Maalse Steenweg 2, 8310 Sint-Kruis, tel. +32 (0)50 68 77 88, www.timothygoffin.be (15/20 graded by GaultMillau)
- » **Patrick Devos**   Zilverstraat 41, 8000 Brugge, tel. +32 (0)50 33 55 66, www.patrickdevos.be (15/20 graded by GaultMillau)
- » **Refter**   Molenmeers 2, 8000 Brugge, tel. +32 (0)50 44 49 00, www.bistrorefter.be (14/20 graded by GaultMillau and rising Star according to Bib Gourmand)
- » **Bonte B**   Dweersstraat 12, 8000 Brugge, tel. +32 (0)50 34 83 43, www.restaurantbonteb.be (14/20 graded by GaultMillau)
- » **Bruut**   Meestraat 9, 8000 Brugge, tel. +32 (0)50 69 55 09, www.bistrobruut.be (14/20 graded by GaultMillau)
- » **La Tâche**   Blankenbergse Steenweg 1, 8000 Sint-Pieters, tel. +32 (0)50 68 02 52, www.latache.be (14/20 graded by GaultMillau)
- » **Le Manoir Quatre Saisons**   Heilige-Geeststraat 1, 8000 Brugge, tel. +32 (0)50 34 30 01, www.castillion.be (14/20 graded by GaultMillau)
- » **Less**   Torhoutse Steenweg 479, 8200 Sint-Michiels, tel. +32 (0)50 69 93 69, www.l-e-s-s.be (14/20 graded by GaultMillau)
- » **'t Pandreitje**   Pandreitje 6, 8000 Brugge, tel. +32 (0)50 33 11 90, www.pandreitje.be (14/20 graded by GaultMillau)
- » **Rock Fort**   Langestraat 15, 8000 Brugge, tel. +32 (0)50 33 41 13, www.rock-fort.be (14/20 graded by GaultMillau)
- » **Tanuki**   Oude Gentweg 1, 8000 Brugge, tel. +32 (0)50 34 75 12, www.tanuki.be (14/20 graded by GaultMillau)
- » **Tête Pressée**   Koningin Astridlaan 100, 8200 Sint-Michiels, tel. +32 (0)470 21 26 27, www.tetepressee.be (14/20 graded by GaultMillau and Rising Star according to Bib Gourmand)
- » **Assiette Blanche**   Philipstockstraat 23-25, 8000 Brugge, tel. +32 (0)50 34 00 94, www.assietteblanche.be (13/20 graded by GaultMillau and Rising Star according to Bib Gourmand)

» **Burg 9**  Burg 9, 8000 Brugge, tel. +32 (0)50 33 35 99, www.burg9.be
(13/20 graded by GaultMillau)

» **Bhavani**  Simon Stevinplein 5, 8000 Brugge, tel. +32 (0)50 33 90 25,
www.bhavani.be (13/20 graded by GaultMillau)

» **De Mangerie**  Oude Burg 20, 8000 Brugge, tel. +32 (0)50 33 93 36,
www.mangerie.com (13/20 graded by GaultMillau)

» **De Visscherie**  Vismarkt 8, 8000 Brugge, tel. +32 (0)50 33 02 12,
www.visscherie.be (13/20 graded by GaultMillau)

» **Lieven**  Philipstockstraat 45, 8000 Brugge, tel. +32 (0)50 68 09 75,
www.etenbijlieven.be (13/20 graded by GaultMillau)

» **Weinebrugge**  Leikendreef 1, 8200 Sint-Michiels, tel. +32 (0)50 38 44 40,
www.weinebrugge.be (13/20 graded by GaultMillau)

» **'t Zwaantje**  Gentpoortvest 70, 8000 Brugge, tel. +32 (0)473 71 25 80,
www.hetzwaantje.be (13/20 graded by GaultMillau)

» **De Florentijnen**  Academiestraat 1, 8000 Brugge, tel. +32 (0)50 67 75 33,
www.deflorentijnen.be (Rising Star according to GaultMillau)

» **Duc de Bourgogne**  Huidenvettersplein 12, 8000 Brugge, tel. +32 (0)50 33 20 38,
www.ducdebourgogne.be (Rising Star according to GaultMillau)

» **Huyze Die Maene**  Markt 17, 8000 Brugge, tel. +32 (0)50 33 39 59,
www.huyzediemaene.be (Rising Star according to GaultMillau)

» **'t Jong Gerecht**  Langestraat 119, 8000 Brugge, tel. +32 (0)50 31 32 32,
www.tjonggerecht.be (Rising Star according to GaultMillau)

» **Kwizien Divien**  Hallestraat 4, 8000 Brugge, tel. +32 (0)50 34 71 29,
www.kwiziendivien.be (Rising Star according to GaultMillau)

» **Parkrestaurant**  Minderbroedersstraat 1, 8000 Brugge, tel. +32 (0)497 80 18 72,
www.parkrestaurant.be (Rising Star according to GaultMillau)

» **'t Apertje**  Damse Vaart-Zuid 223, 8310 Sint-Kruis, tel. +32 (0)50 35 00 12,
www.apertje.be (Rising Star according to Bib Gourmand)

» **Kok au Vin**  Ezelstraat 21, 8000 Brugge, tel. +32 (0)50 33 95 21,
www.kok-au-vin.be (Rising Star according to Bib Gourmand)

» **Kurt's Pan**  Sint-Jakobsstraat 58, 8000 Brugge, tel. +32 (0)50 34 12 24,
www.kurtspan.be (Rising Star according to Bib Gourmand)

» **Pergola**  Meestraat 7, 8000 Brugge, tel. +32 (0)50 44 76 50,
www.restaurantpergola.be (Rising Star according to Bib Gourmand)

*More tips on finding the right address for you can be found in the section 'Tips from Bruges
connoisseurs'. Pages 108-109, 116-117, 124-125, 132-133, 140-141*

# Shopping in Bruges

Bruges has lots of shops to offer you something special: authentic places that surprise you again and again with their clever and original products. The city guarantees a harmonious mix of creative boutiques, trendy newcomers and classic names that have been professionally managed by the same family for generations.

## Where to shop?

Because Bruges is pedestrian-friendly and the main streets are all close to each other, a day's shopping here is much more relaxing than in many other cities. You will find all the major national and international chains, as well as trendy local boutiques. And if you leave the beaten shopping paths you will certainly make plenty of interesting new discoveries. The most important shopping streets (indicated in yellow on the removable city map) run between the Market Square and the old city gates: Steenstraat, Simon Stevinplein, Mariastraat, Zuidzandstraat, Sint-Jakobsstraat, Sint-Amandsstraat, Geldmuntstraat, Noordzandstraat, Smedenstraat, Vlamingstraat, Philipstockstraat, Academiestraat, Hoogstraat, Langestraat and the Katelijnestraat. There is also a small but elegant shopping centre, the Zilverpand, hidden between the Noordzandstraat and the Zuidzandstraat. Each neighbourhood has its own unique atmosphere. In the Steenstraat, for example, you will find the famous brand names, whereas the Langestraat boasts many little second-hand and bric-à-brac shops. The large hypermarkets are located just outside the city centre. You don't know where to start? On www.visitbruges.be there is a selection of well-established family businesses and creative entrepreneurs. These are all unique boutiques, situated close to the city centre, and each guaranteed to give you a great shopping experience.

## Off to the market

There is nothing quite as delightful as shopping at a local market. In Bruges, this is possible almost every day. On Wednesday there is a food market on the Market Square from 8.00 a.m. to 1.30 p.m.  On Saturday (8.00 a.m.–1.30 p.m.) the Zand Square and the Beursplein are taken over by a large food and general market (flowers, animals, clothing, etc.). And on Sunday, from 7.00 a.m. to 2.00 p.m., you can visit the food and general market on the Veemarkt, near the Koningin Astridlaan in the Sint-Michiels district. Every morning (8.00 a.m.–1.30 p.m.) from Tuesday to Saturday, you can buy fresh fish and fish dishes at the Vismarkt (Fish Market). Finally, during the weekends and on public holidays from mid-March to mid-November, you can browse at the second-hand and craft market along the Dijver (10.00 a.m.–6.00 p.m.). If you love old bric-à-brac and antiques, you should definitely visit the 'Zandfeesten', the largest second-hand and craft market in Belgium, which is organized three times each summer (in early July, early August and late September) on the Zand Square and in the Koning Albertpark. *(Also see page 17)*

## Souvenirs

### LACE

Do you want a souvenir that is a little bit out of the ordinary? What about a unique piece of Bruges lace? You will be buying fine hand-made craftsmanship with a

cast iron reputation, available in the city's many top-quality lace shops. These lace ambassadors have something to suit every taste: from valuable antique pieces to hip, modern creations that are much in demand with today's young fashion designers. Since time immemorial, Bruges and lace have been inextricably linked. The deft hands of thousands of women and girls earned Bruges lace worldwide fame. At one time, a quarter of all the women in Bruges were lace-makers. Even nowadays, it is still possible to see traditional Bruges lace-makers at work in some of the lace shops. Just watch those bobbins fly! Or would you rather have a go yourself? The new Lace Museum offers courses (prior registration necessary), where experienced and enthusiastic lace-makers will teach you the finest tricks of the trade.
*You can learn more about lace and the Lace Centre on p. 83-84 and in the interview with Kumiko Nakazaki (page 128).*

### BEER

People from Bruges like to drink a beer or two every now and then, especially when it is brewed in their own city. That is why Bruges can boast a number of typical city beers: the Straffe Hendrik and the Brugse Zot are brewed in the Halve Maan Brewery, located in the heart of the historic city centre, while the Fort Lapin 8 triple and the Fort Lapin 10 quadruple are produced in the Fort Lapin Brewery on the outskirts of the city. These beers are not your average, everyday beers, but are artisanal products full of quality and character. And well worth taking home to share with your family and friends! Are you convinced? Then why not come back for the annual Bruges Beer Festival or visit the brand-new Bruges Beer Museum on the Markt (Market Square).
*You can read more about the Bruges Beer Festival on page 95, about the Halve Maan Brewery on page 76 and about the Bruges Beer Museum on page 77. Visit www. visitbruges.be to discover the city's very best beer addresses.*

## DIAMONDS

As early as the 14<sup>th</sup> century, Bruges already had an important diamond trade. The technique for cutting diamonds on a rotating disk was invented in Bruges around 1476 by local goldsmith Lodewijk van Berquem. A year later, Emperor Maximilian of Austria proposed to Mary of Burgundy by offering her the first diamond engagement ring in history. In the Diamond Laboratory at the Bruges Diamond Museum you can watch how experts professionally cut and polish all that sparkling splendour. Perhaps you might even find some shining inspiration of your own. Armed with this inspiration, you will then be able to assess the museum shop and the many other fine jewellery stores in the city with a keen expert's eye in order to pick out the very best bargains!

*For more detailed information on the Bruges Diamond Museum, see page 79.*

## CHOCOLATE

A professional chocolate guild, a special city chocolate (the Bruges Swan), a fascinating chocolate museum and even a delightful chocolate walk. What more do you need to convince you that Bruges is the capital of the Belgian chocolate industry? Bruges still has more than 50 excellent chocolate boutiques, catering for all tastes. Delicious old-fashioned block chocolate; wonderfully scrumptious pralines that really are finger-licking good; ingenious molecular chocolate preparations made to measure for the city's star-rated chefs: the chocolate-makers of Bruges can do it all!

*An overview of the city's finest chocolate addresses is served on www.visitbruges. be. Read more about chocolate on page 78.*

The Beguinage

# Walking in
# **Bruges**

# Walk 1

## Bruges,
## proud World Heritage City

Bruges may be, quite rightly, very proud of her World Heritage status, but the city is happily embracing the future too! This walk takes you along world-famous panoramic views, sky-high monuments and centuries-old squares invigorated by contemporary constructions. One foot planted in the Middle Ages, the other one firmly planted in the present. This walk is an absolute must for first-time visitors who would like to explore the very heart of the city straight away. Keep your camera at the ready!

MARKT

BURG

Park Sebrechts

Sint-Jakobs-plein

FINISH

OUD SINT-JAN
Congrescentrum

BEGIJNHOF

STATION

**WALK 1**

» START
ℹ 't Zand
(Concertgebouw)

» DISTANCE
3 km

» FINISH
Saint John's Hospital

## From 't Zand to Simon Stevinplein

This walk starts at the Tourist office 🅸 't Zand (Concertgebouw).

't Zand is dominated by the concert hall **16**, one of Bruges' most talked-about buildings. Clear-cut proof that this World Heritage city isn't afraid of the future. On the very top floor of this modern cube-shaped building you can find the Sound Factory **42**. Don't forget to drop in at 🅸 't Zand (Concertgebouw) on the ground floor: here you will find all the necessary tourist information as well as expert advice on all cultural events.

Leave 🅸 't Zand (Concertgebouw) behind you, walk along the square and turn into Zuidzandstraat, the first street on the right. Saint Saviour's Cathedral **23** looms up ahead on your right after three hundred metres. Bruges' oldest parish church is located on a lower level than the present Zuidzandstraat, which is situated on an old sand ridge. What's more, in the Middle Ages people simply threw their refuse out onto the street where it was then flattened by passing carts and coaches. This raised the street level still further. Inside Saint Saviour's, the church tower's wooden rafters can be lit. The cathedral treasury displays, amongst others, interesting copper memorial plaques, fine examples of gold and silver and paintings by Dieric Bouts, Hugo van der Goes and Pieter Pourbus.

> TIP
>
> Why not call in at the Sound Factory and let those Bruges bells ring! And because the Sound Factory is located at the very top of the Concert Hall, you can enjoy a superb panorama over the city while the bells play your very own carillon composition.

Continue past the cathedral and walk down Sint-Salvatorskerkhof immediately on the right. Turn left into Sint-Salvatorskoorstraat. The Simon Stevinplein opens up at the end of this street. This attractive square, lined with cosy restaurant terraces in summertime, is named after Simon Stevin, a well-

known Flemish-Dutch scientist. His gracious statue naturally takes centre stage.

## Markt and Burg

Continue down Oude Burg, a street in the right-hand corner of the square. Before long you will see the Cloth Halls **10** on your left. These belong to the Belfry **04**. You're allowed to cross the halls' imposing inner court between 8.00 a.m. and 6.00 p.m. during the week, and between 9.00 a.m. to 6.00 p.m. on Saturday. The Markt is at the other end of the yard. If the gate is closed, turn back and walk down Hallestraat, which runs parallel to the Halls.

*Walk 2 (see page 43, 44 and 45) comments extensively on Markt.*

Return to the Belfry **04** and walk down Breidelstraat, a traffic-free alley on the corner. Continue to Burg. Along the way on your right you will notice De Garre, a narrow alley. This may be the narrowest street in Bruges (try walking side by side here!), it nevertheless boasts a fair number of cosy cafés. Burg is the most majestic square in the city, so take your time to admire its grandeur. The main character in this medieval story is the City Hall **09** **43** (1376-1420), one of the oldest city halls in the Netherlands and a Gothic example for all its brothers and sisters that were built later, from Louvain to Audenarde and Brussels. Having admired its exterior, enter the impressive Gothic Hall and gaze in admiration at the polychrome floating ribs of the vaulted ceiling. Hiding on the right-hand side of this Gothic monument is the Basilica of the Holy Blood **01**. It was originally dedi-

## BURG: AN ARCHITECTURAL SYNOPSIS

Art lovers have already noticed that Burg projects a wonderful cross-section of stunning architectural styles. It is, indeed, a summing-up in one place of all the styles that have caught our imagination throughout the various centuries.

From Romanesque (Saint Basil's Church) and Gothic (City Hall) by way of Renaissance (Civil Registry) and Baroque (Deanery) to Classicism (Mansion of the Liberty of Bruges). There's no need to go and dash all around Bruges to see it all!

01

cated to both Our Lady and Saint Basil, and was built as a fortress church on two levels between 1139 and 1157. The lower church, hidden away behind the Gothic Saint Ivo's Chapel, has retained its Romanesque character. The upper chapel, which was originally little more than a kind of balcony, was gradually extended over the years to become a church in its own right. It was only during the 19th century that it was renovated in Neo-Gothic style that can be seen today. The sacred relic of the Holy Blood has been kept here since the 13th century. Each year on Ascension Day, the reliquary is carried along in the Procession of the Holy Blood, a much-loved event that has been warming the hearts of the entire population from as early as 1304. Facing the basilica is the gleaming Renaissance façade of the erstwhile Civil Registry **03** (1534-1537, which now houses the City Archive **08** adjacent to the Liberty of Bruges **01** **14**. Its showpiece is a splendid oak mantelpiece with an alabaster frieze (1529). Adjoining is the former mansion of the Liberty

of Bruges (1722-1727). It is from here that the country around Bruges was administered. After 1795 a court of justice was installed. It has been the city's administrative centre since 1988. Once upon a time Saint Donatian's Cathedral graced the spot directly in front of the City Hall. The church was torn down in 1799. Adjacent to it is the Deanery (1655-1666) **17**. It is still possible to see the foundations of the old cathedral in the cellar of the Crown Plaza Hotel.

## Fishy stories

Proceed to Blinde-Ezelstraat, the little street to the left of the City Hall. Don't forget to look back at the lovely arch between City Hall and Old Civil Registry **03** **08**. Do you see Solomon? Left of him is the statue of Prosperity, to the right the statue of Peace.

According to tradition, Blinde-Ezelstraat (Blind Donkey Street) owes its name to a tavern of the same name. The house in the left hand corner hugging the water used to house a mill driven by

pose in 1821, fresh seafood was sold, a delicacy that only the rich could afford. Today you can still buy your fresh saltwater fish here every morning from Tuesday to Saturday.

Retrace your steps and turn left in front of the bridge towards Huidenvettersplein.

Whereas the Vismarkt served the rich, Huidenvettersplein (Tanners Square) served the poor. No sea fish on the menu here, but affordable freshwater fish. The post in the middle of the square used to have a twin brother: in between the two posts hung the scales that the fish were weighed on. The large, striking building dominating the square used to be the meeting hall of the tanners. Here they sold the cow hides that they had turned into leather. Since tanning was a rather smelly job, it is no coincidence that the tanners' hall adjoined the fish market. Look out for the statuette adorning the corner of the hall. It is no surprise that the little fellow raises his nose.

a donkey. In order to preserve the poor animal from the depressing thought that the only thing it had to do was turn endless rounds, a blindfold was put on the donkey. A new street name was born. Look left on the bridge: Meebrug is said to be the oldest bridge in Bruges.

The Vismarkt 22 opens up immediately past the bridge.

At first, fish was sold on one of the Markt's corners, but as the townspeople complained about the stench, the fishmongers were forced to move and sell their wares here. In the covered arcade, specially erected for the pur-

Huidenvettersplein

Continue to Rozenhoedkaai.
Keep right.
Rozenhoedkaai is the most photographed spot in Bruges. So, take out your camera! This used to be the salt port. In the Middle Ages salt was as expensive as gold: it served to preserve food and to season dishes. A word like *salaris* (Dutch), *salaire* (French), salary still harks back to medieval times. The word derives from *sal*, which is Latin for salt.

## From Groeninge to the Bonifacius Bridge

Continue along Dijver.
In the middle of the 11th century, the hermit Everelmus built a prayer chapel on Dijver. Along this atmospheric stretch of water, you will first find the College of Europe (numbers 9 to 11) **03**, an international postgraduate institution that focuses on European affairs, and then the Groeninge Museum **25**, Bruges' most renowned museum. On display are world-famous masterpieces by Jan van Eyck, Hans Memling, Hugo van der Goes, Gerard David and many other Flemish primitives. The museum also has a valuable collection of Flemish expressionists, neoclassical top notch paintings from the 18th and 19th centuries and post-war modern art. Overall, the museum shows a complete overview of Belgian and southern Dutch (Flemish) painting from the 15th to the 20th century. The museum entrance is reached through a few picturesque courtyard gardens.

---

### 🏠 ALMSHOUSES, THE QUICKEST WAY TO HEAVEN

These charitable dwellings were built from the 14th century onwards. They were sometimes set up by the guilds to lodge their elderly members, and sometimes by widows or well-to-do burghers who wanted to ensure their place in heaven. For that purpose, each set of almshouses had its own chapel where the occupants of the almshouses would be expected  to send their prayers of thanks up to heaven. Practically all of the almshouses have been carefully restored and modernised and offer cosy living to today's elderly, whilst their small yet picturesque gardens and white-painted façades offer welcoming peace and quiet to the present-day visitor. Feel free to enter these premises, but don't forget to respect their perfect tranquillity.

*(On the City map the Almshouses are indicated by 🏠)*

*Would you like to find out more about the Flemish primitives? Then leaf through to the interview on page 120 with Till-Holger Borchert, the Groeninge Museum's chief curator.*

Continue along Dijver. The entrance gate to the Gruuthuse Museum **26** is on your left just beyond the little bridge.
This museum is closed for restoration until 2018.

Continue to Guido Gezelleplein, then turn left in front of the Church of Our Lady **15** **34** and follow the narrow footpath to the picturesque Bonifacius Bridge.
The crosses that you see all over the place don't belong to graves at all – they are crosses taken down from church steeples during the First World War to disorientate the enemy spies. The crosses have never been put up again. Close to the Bonifacius Bridge is Bru-

ges' smallest Gothic window. Look up! It was through this window that the lords and ladies of Gruuthuse were able to peer down onto their private jetty.
Across the bridge is the charming city garden 'Arentshof' of the Arentshuis **02**, an elegant 18th-century abode. The top floor houses work by the versatile British artist Frank Brangwyn. The ground floor is reserved for temporary exhibitions. Rik Poot's (1924-2006) remarkable sculpture group in the garden represents the *Horsemen of the Apocalypse*: famine, death, revolution and the plague. A theme that appealed to the painter Hans Memling as well. Go through the garden gate to reach the Groeninge Museum **25**, where more work by Memling is displayed.

## On to the Beguinage!

Leave the garden once more through the narrow garden gate and turn left into Groeninge, a winding street. Turn right again at the intersection with Nieuwe Gentweg. Notice the Saint Joseph (17th century) and the De Meulenaere almshouses (1613). Continue down the street.

On the left-hand corner of Oude Gentweg and Katelijnestraat is the Diamond Museum **20**, Bruges' most glittering museum and the place to be for all lovers of bling. It goes without saying that an inspiring diamond museum simply couldn't be absent in the most romantic city of the western hemisphere!

Wijngaardplein

Turn left into Katelijnestraat, then immediately right into Wijngaardstraat. Cross Wijngaardplein – a stopping place for coachmen. A little further on turn right onto the bridge beside the Sashuis (lock house) to enter the Beguinage. The bridge offers a fine view of the Minnewater.

The Minnewater used to be the landing stage of the barges or track boats that provided a regular connection between Bruges and Ghent. Today it is one of Bruges' most romantic beauty spots. Equally atmospheric, yet of a totally different nature, is the Beguinage. Although the 'Princely Beguinage Ten Wijngaarde' **02** **02**, founded in 1245, is no longer occupied by beguines (single lay women who formed their own religious community), but by nuns of the Order of Saint Benedict, you can still form an excellent picture of what daily life looked like in the 17th century at the Beguine's house **03**. The imposing courtyard garden, the white-painted house fronts and blessed peace create an atmosphere all of its own. The entrance gate closes each day at 6.30 p.m. without fail. You have been warned!

Walk around the Beguinage and leave through the main gate. Turn left after the bridge and left again to reach Walplein.

De Halve Maan **11**, a brewery established as early as 1564, is at number 26 (at your left hand side). This is Bruges' last active city brewery. Their speciality

is 'Brugse Zot' (Bruges' Fool), a spirited top-fermented beer made from malt, hop and special yeast. The name of the beer refers to the nickname of the Bruges townspeople, a name allegedly conferred upon them by Maximilian of Austria. In order to welcome the duke, the citizens paraded past him in a lavish procession of brightly coloured merrymakers and fools. When a short time later they asked their ruler to finance a new 'zothuis' or madhouse, his answer was as short as it was forceful: 'The only people I have seen here are fools. Bruges is one big madhouse. Just close the gates!'

## A splendid finish at Saint John's Hospital

Turn left into Zonnekemeers. Once across the water, turn right to enter the area of Old Saint John via the car park.

The former Hospital of Saint John (13th– 14th centuries) **38** has a proud eight century-long history. The oldest documents even date back to the 12th century! Here, nuns and monks took good care of pilgrims, travellers and the sick. And people sometimes chose to die here. Hans Memling once was a patient here too. According to a much later legend, he rewarded his benefactors with no fewer than six masterpieces. Right in front of the convent buildings of the old hospital complex you will come across *The Veins of the Convent*, a sculptural work by the contemporary Italian artist Giuseppe Penone. Or how history still feeds the present – what could be more appropriate for a World Heritage City like Bruges! Turn left at the corner and then go immediately right: in the open space of the courtyard you will find the herb garden and the entrance to the 17th century pharmacy, which is well worth a visit. The herb garden contains all the necessary ingredients for 'gruut' or 'gruit', including lady's mantle, myrtle and laurel. You can find an explanation of what *gruut* is in *walk 2 on page 42.*

Retrace your steps, turn left and walk-through the passage. The entrance to the imposing medieval hospital wards, its church, the Diksmuide attic and the old dormitory are just around the corner to the right.

# Walk 2
# Bruges: B of Burgundian

When, during Bruges' Golden Age Philip the Bold, Duke of Burgundy, married Margaret of Dampierre, the daughter of the last Count of Flanders, the county of Flanders suddenly found itself belonging to Burgundy. As the Burgundian court liked to stay in Bruges, the port city became a magnet for noblemen, merchants and artists. They naturally all wanted to get their share of the city's wealth. Today the Burgundian influence is still strongly felt throughout Bruges. Let's discover a northern city with a southern character.

## WALK 2

» START
Guido Gezelleplein,
Church of Our Lady

» DISTANCE
2,5 km

» FINISH
Prinsenhof

## From Guido Gezelleplein to Markt

This square is named after the Flemish priest and poet Guido Gezelle (1830-1899). Take a seat on one of the square's benches and enjoy Gezelle's lovely statue and the side-view of the Church of Our Lady . Its one hundred and fifteen (and a half!)-metre high brick tower is sure proof of the craftsmanship of Bruges' artisans. The church is currently undergoing large-scale renovation work, so that it is not possible to admire all its many fine works of art. However, Michelangelo's world-famous *Madonna and Child* can still be viewed. On your left is the striking residence of the lords of Gruut-huse, now the Gruuthuse Museum This, too, is undergoing renovation and will be closed until 2018. The tower and well (which unfortunately cannot be seen from the Guido Gezelleplein) were status symbols, and evidence of the

Gruuthuse family's great wealth. They made their fortune from their exclusive rights on 'gruut', a herb mixture that, ages before hop, was used to flavour beer. Louis of Gruuthuse not only com-manded the army of Charles the Bold, he was also the personal bodyguard to Mary of Burgundy. A cultured man, he owned the Gruuthuse manuscript, a famous medieval codex containing amongst its many texts no fewer than 147 songs. The family's motto was *Plus est en vous* (There is more in you than

you think). It's proudly displayed above the door of their residence.

**Continue along the narrow footpath to the left of the church.**
Look up immediately beyond the bend. Do you see the chapel that seems to hold the Gruuthuse Museum and the Church of Our Lady in a close embrace? As the lords of Gruuthuse were far too grand to mingle with the populace, they had their own private chapel high above the street, where they could follow Mass. This intimate place of worship can still be visited.

**Retrace your steps, cross the attractive Gruuthuseplein and turn right into Dijver.**
Number 12 is the Groeninge Museum 25, Bruges' most famous museum. *An interview with chief curator Till-Holger Borchert is on page 120.* Further along Dijver is one of the locations of the College of Europe 03, numbers 9-11, an international postgraduate institution that focuses on Europe.

**Carry on down Dijver and turn left into Wollestraat.**
Perez de Malvenda 13 is an impressive mansion on the corner of Wollestraat. This 15th-16th century town house, now a food shop, has been restored from attic to cellar. Just before Markt are the Cloth Halls 10, the Belfry's 04 warehouses and sales outlets. Facing the street, countless stalls were selling all sorts of herbs for medicinal purpose and potions. Indeed, Bruges being an important trading centre could by then import and sell a variety of herbs from all over Europe.

# Markt, Bruges' beating heart

**Wollestraat leads to Markt.**
Markt is dominated by its Belfry 04, for centuries the city's foremost edifice and the perfect lookout in case of war, fire or any other calamity. You can still climb to the top of the tower; but you will need to conquer no fewer than 366 steps to get there! Fortunately, there are a couple of places during your

## THE CORRECT TIME

A gleaming terrestrial globe proudly sits on top of Boechoute, the house on the corner. This late Gothic (15th century) building with its screen gable is now the Meridian 3 tearoom. When the Brussels to Bruges railway line was inaugurated, not all clocks in Belgium were set to the same time. The shortcoming was cured by this globe. At noon exactly, the sun coincided with its shadow through a hole in the globe. The line that was thus drawn can still be traced today thanks to a string of copper nails.

Markt

ascent where you can stop for a breather. Once at the top you will be rewarded with an unforgettable panoramic view. At the foot of the Belfry are the world's most famous chippies ('frietkoten')! The statue of Jan Breydel and Pieter de Coninck graces the middle of the square. These two popular heroes of Bruges resisted French oppression and consequently played an important part during the Battle of the Golden Spurs in 1302. Their statue neatly looks out onto

## TIP

As you are climbing your way to the top of the belfry tower, why not stop for a break at the vaulted treasure chamber, where the city's charters, seal and public funds were all kept during medieval times. You can make a second stop at the 'Stenen Vloer' (Stone Floor): here you will learn

The drum

everything you ever wanted to know about the clock, the drum and the carillon of 47 harmonious bells, which together weigh a staggering 27 tons of pure bronze. If you are really lucky, you might see the carilloneur in action, banging on the wooden keys that make the bells sound.

*(Also read the interview with carilloneur Frank Deleu on page 104)*

the Gothic revival style Provincial Court (Markt 3) .

Until the 18th century this was the place – now occupied by the Post Office, the Historium **27** and the Bruges Beer Museum **13** – where proudly stood the Water Halls (Waterhalle), a covered warehouse where goods were loaded and unloaded along the river that ran alongside the square. Today the river is still there, but now runs through a series of underground vaults.

Would you like a break? Then treat yourself to a coach ride and explore the city by horse and carriage for half an hour. Or maybe you prefer a fifty-minute city tour by minibus *[See page 68]*? You can continue your walk after your trip.

*See page 68]*

## From Markt to Jan van Eyckplein

Ignore Markt on your left and continue straight ahead to Vlamingstraat. In the 13th century, this used to be the harbour area's shopping street. A fair number of banks had a branch here, and wine taverns were two a penny. Each of these had (and still has) a deep cellar where French and Rhenish wines could easily be stacked. In the medieval vaulted cellars of Taverne Curiosa (Vlamingstraat 22), the alcoholic atmosphere of those bygone days can still be inhaled. Halfway along Vlamingstraat is the elegant City Theatre **44** on your left. This royal theatre (1869) is one of Europe's best-preserved city theatres. Behind the Neo-Renaissance façade lie a magnificent auditorium and a

TIP

Since as long ago as 1897, two green painted mobile chippies have stood in front of the Belfry. It is definitely the best place in town to buy – and sell – chips, good for the annual consumption of several tons of fast food! The city's chip-sellers can bid once every two years for the right to stand on this lucrative spot. The highest bidder gets the contract. The stalls are open nearly every hour of the day and night, so that you never need to go hungry!

Vlamingstraat

## SWANS ON THE CANALS

After the death of Mary of Burgundy, Bruges went through some troubled times. The townspeople, enraged by new taxes Maximilian of Austria, Mary's successor, had imposed upon them, rose in revolt against their new ruler. As Maximilian was locked up in House Craenenburg on the market square, he helplessly witnessed the torture and eventual beheading of his bailiff and trusted councillor Pieter Lanchals (Long Neck). According to legend, once the duke had regained power, the citizens of Bruges were ordered to keep swans or long necks ('langhalzen') on the canals for all eternity. In fact, swans were already swimming in the moats around Bruges by this time (15th century).

palatial foyer. Papageno, the bird seller from Mozart's opera, *The Magic Flute*, guards the entrance. His score lies scattered on the square opposite.

Continue along Vlamingstraat and turn right into Kortewinkel just before the water.

Somewhat hidden from gazing eyes, Kortewinkel boasts a unique 16th-century wooden house front. It is one of only two left in the city (you will come across the other one further along this walk). Just a few metres on is another delicious discovery at number 10. The Jesuit Monastery **09** has a magnificent hidden courtyard garden. Is its door open? Then walk in and enjoy its heavenly peace.

Kortewinkel turns into Spaanse Loskaai, the home port of the Spanish merchants until the end of the 16th century.
The picturesque bridge on your left is the Augustine Bridge, one of Bruges' oldest specimens, with its seven hundred summers. The stone seats were originally intended to display the wares of the diligent sellers. The bridge affords an excellent view of the house in

the right-hand corner, which connects Spanjaardstraat with Kortewinkel. This was once the House of God's Succour but is also said to be a haunted house, according to the locals. When an amorous monk was rejected by a nun, the man murdered her and then committed suicide. Ever since they have been haunting that ramshackle building…

**Continue along Spaanse Loskaai, go down the first street on your right and proceed to Oosterlingenplein.**
During Bruges' Golden Age this was the fixed abode of the so-called 'Oosterlingen' or German merchants. Their imposing warehouse took up the entire left side of the square. Today the only remnant is the building to the right of Hotel Bryghia. Their warehouse must have been truly grand!

**Beyond Oosterlingenplein is Woensdagmarkt. You will then find yourself on the square on which the statue of the painter Hans Memling attracts all attention. Turn right into Genthof.**
Here the second of two authentic medieval wooden house fronts draws attention. Notice that each floor juts out a little more than the next one. This building technique, which helped to avoid water damage (but also created extra space), was consequently used in various architectural styles.

# Burgundian Manhattan

**Proceed to Jan van Eyckplein.**
This was Burgundian Bruges' Manhattan, the place to be! Here ships docked, cargoes were loaded and unloaded and tolls were levied. In this unremitting hustle and bustle a cacophony of languages was heard above the din, the one sounding even louder than the other. What a soundtrack! Each business transaction required a few local sounds too, of course, as there always had to be a Bruges broker present who would naturally pocket his cut. On the corner 16th-century Huis De Roode Steen (number 8) has been sparkling in all its glory since its restoration (financed with a subsidy from the city) in 1877. At numbers 1-2 is the Old Tollhouse (1477) **06** **21**, where all tollage was settled. To the left of this monumental building is Pijndershuisje, Bruges' narrowest dwelling. This is where the 'pijnders' or dockworkers used to meet. You can guess the origin of the name by looking at the facade; but you need to look carefully!

---

TIP

The Genthof has in recent years attracted a variety of different arts and crafts. There is a glass-blower, a trendy vintage store and a number of contemporary art galleries. And on the corner you can find 't Terrastje, the café with probably the smallest terrace in Bruges.

---

The hunched 'pijnders' were employed to load and unload sacks and casks.

Continue along Academiestraat. Right on the corner with Jan van Eyck-plein is another remarkable building, distinguished by its striking tower. This is Burghers' Lodge , a kind of 15th century private club where members of the Bruges Bear Company came to meet. Hidden in a niche of this Burghers Lodge is the Bruges' Bear, now one of the city's most important symbols.

Proceed to Grauwwerkersstraat. The little square connecting Academie-straat with Grauwwerkersstraat has been known as 'Beursplein' since time immemorial.
Here merchants were engaged in high-quality trade. The merchant houses of

Genoa (later renamed 'Saaihalle' 08, and today Belgian Fries Museum 22), Florence (now De Florentijnen restaurant) and Venice once stood here side by side like brothers. In front of Huis ter Beurze (1276), the central inn 11, merchants from all over Europe used to gather to arrange business appoint-ments and conduct exchange transac-tions. The Dutch word for stock exchange became 'beurs', derived from the name of the house. Many other languages would take over this term, such as French (*bourse*) or Italian (*borsa*).

Turn into Grauwwerkersstraat and stop immediately in your tracks. The side wall of Huis ter Beurze 11, and more precisely the part between the two sets of ground-floor windows, bears the signatures of the stonecut-

## THE LITTLE BEAR OF BRUGES

When Baldwin Iron Arm, the first Count of Flanders, visited Bruges for the first time, the first creature he saw was a big 'white' bear. According to the legend, all this happened in the 9th century. After a fierce fight the count succeeded in killing the animal. In homage to the courageous beast, he proclaimed the bear to be the city's very own symbol. Today 'Bruges' oldest inhabitant' in the niche of the Burghers Lodge is festively rigged out during exceptional celebrations. The Bruges Bear is holding the coat of arms of the Noble Company of the White Bear, which was a kind of jousting club for local knights, founded shortly after Baldwin's famous victory over the original 'white' bear.

ters. This way everybody knew which mason cut which stones and how much each mason had to be paid. The house next-door to Huis ter Beurze, called the

Little Beurze, still sits on its original street level.

**Turn left into Naaldenstraat.**
On your right, Bladelin Court **09** with its attractive tower looms up ahead. In the 15th century, Pieter Bladelin, portrayed above the gate whilst praying to the Virgin Mary, leased his house to the Florentine banking family of de' Medici, who set up one of their branches here. Today the edifice belongs to the Sisters of Our Lady of Seven Sorrows. We highly recommend a visit. But make a reservation before you go, by phoning +32 (0)50 33 64 34 and admire the magnificent courtyard garden and the city's first Renaissance façade, embellished with two stone medallions representing Lorenzo de' Medici and his wife Clarissa Orsini.

## PRINSENHOF GOSSIP

> As Philip the Good hadn't yet laid eyes on his future wife, he sent Jan van Eyck to Portugal to paint her portrait. This way the duke wanted to make certain he had made the right choice. The duke's ploy worked, because history teaches us that the couple had a happy marriage.

> Although the popular Mary of Burgundy incurred only seemingly minor injuries as a result of a fall with her horse, the accident would eventually lead to her death from a punctured lung at Prinsenhof. Back in those times there was no cure for inflammation.

> During the hotel renovation no fewer than 568 silver coins, minted between 1755 and 1787, were dug up. After some careful counting and calculations it is assumed that the energetic English nuns, who lived there at that time, entrusted the coins to the soil so as to prevent the advancing French troops from stealing their hard-earned capital.

Somewhat further along, next to another ornamental tower, turn right into Boterhuis, a winding cobbled alley that catapults you back straight into the Middle Ages. Keep right, pass Saint James' Church and turn left into Moerstraat.

The Dukes of Burgundy and the vast majority of foreign merchants patronised Saint James' Church **22**. Their extravagant gifts have left their glittering mark on the interior.

## Prinsenhof (the Princes 'Court), home base of the Dukes of Burgundy

Turn left into Geerwijnstraat and carry on to Muntplein.

Muntplein (Coin Square) belongs to nearby Prinsenhof **16**. As you might

have guessed, this was where Bruges' mint was situated. The statue *Flandria Nostra* (Our Flanders), which represents a noblewoman on horseback, was designed by the Belgian sculptor Jules Lagae (1862-1931).

Muntpoort

**16**

At the end of Geerwijnstraat turn right into Geldmuntstraat. The walk's finishing point is Prinsenhof.

We end the walk on a highlight. Prinsenhof used to be the palace of the counts and dukes. This impressive mansion, originally seven times the size of what you see today, was expanded in the 15th century by Philip the Good to celebrate his (third) marriage to Isabella of Portugal. When Charles the Bold remarried Margaret of York, one of the largest bathhouses in Europe, a game court (to play 'jeu de paume' or the palm game, the forerunner of tennis) and a zoological garden were all added to the ducal residence. It is no surprise that Prinsenhof not only became the favourite pied-à-terre of

TIP

Whoever wants to get a really good impression of the magnificence of this city castle and its elegant gardens should follow the signs in the Ontvangersstraat to the hotel car park at Moerstraat 27. Of course, you can always treat yourself – and your nearest and dearest – to a princely drink in the bar of the Dukes' Palace Hotel: the perfect way to enjoy the grandeur and luxury of the complex.

the Dukes of Burgundy, but also the nerve centre of their political, economic and cultural ambitions. Both Philip the Good (d.1467) and Mary of Burgundy (d.1482) breathed their last here. After the death of the popular Mary of Burgundy the palace's fortunes declined, until it eventually ended up in private hands. In the 17th century, English nuns converted it into a boarding school for girls of well-to-do parents. Nowadays you can stay in the Prinsenhof Castle in true princely style.

TIP

Behind the street Boterhuis, at Sint-Jakobsstraat 36, you will find Cinema Lumière **09**, purveyor of the better kind of artistic film. In other words, the place to be for real film-lovers.

# Walk 3
# Strolling through silent Bruges

Although the parishes of Saint Anne and Saint Giles are known as places of great tranquillity, the fact that they are off the beaten track does not mean that the visitor will be short of adventure. How about a row of nostalgic windmills? Or perhaps some unpretentious working-class neighbourhoods or a couple of exclusive gentlemen's clubs? Will you be able to absorb all these impressions serenely? Don't worry. After the tour we invite you to catch your breath in Bruges 'oldest cafe!

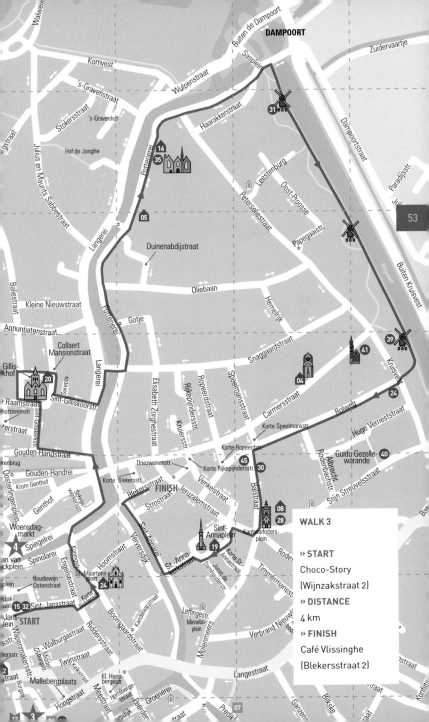

**DAMPOORT**

53

**WALK 3**

» **START**

Choco-Story
(Wijnzakstraat 2)

» **DISTANCE**

4 km

» **FINISH**

Café Vlissinghe
(Blekersstraat 2)

## From Choco-Story to Gouden-Handstraat

Choco-Story (Museum of chocolate) **15** is the perfect starting point for the longest walk in this guide. This museum not only dips you in the yummy history of chocolate and cocoa, it also offers extensive chocolate tasting. If you wish, you can also buy your supplies here. No doubt the chocolate will help you to keep up a brisk pace! At the same address Lumina Domestica **32** contains the world's largest collection of lamps and lights. The museum also houses 6,000 antiques.

Turn left into Sint-Jansstraat, carry onto Korte Riddersstraat and continue until the end of the street.
Saint Walburga's Church **24** rises up in all its magnificence right in front of you. This Baroque edifice (1619-1642) boasts

24

remarkable marble communion rail and high altar. Nearby, at number 3 there is a splendid 18th century mansion.

Continue down Koningstraat to the bridge.
This bridge, which connects poetic Spinolarei with Spiegelrei, affords a lovely view of Oud Huis Amsterdam on your left. Today this historic town house (Spiegelrei 3) is an elegant hotel. This part of the city used to be mainly populated by the English and Scots. The English merchants even had their own 'steegere' or stair where their goods were unloaded. The stair is still there, and the street connecting it is appropriately called Engelsestraat. The dignified white school building (number 15) across the bridge was once a college of English Jesuits.

## Saint Giles', home base of workmen and artists

Cross the bridge, turn right along Spiegelrei and turn into Gouden-Handstraat, the fourth street on your left.

In the 15<sup>th</sup> century Gouden-Hand-straat and the parish of Saint Giles were known as the artists' quarter. Hans Memling may have lived a few streets further down in Sint-Joris-straat; the fact of the matter is that Jan van Eyck had a studio in Gouden-Handstraat, and that his somewhat lesser known fellow artists also used to congregate in this neigh-bourhood.

Turn right into Sint-Gilliskerkstraat. This street bumps into Saint Giles' Church **20** in the heart of the tranquil quarter of Saint Giles'. Initially a cha-pel, this building was upgraded to a pa-rish church in 1258. In spite of its inte-rior in Gothic revival style and its su-perb paintings, the church takes on the appearance of a simple, sturdy village church. Don't be misled. In and around the church countless famous painters were buried, such as Hans Memling (d.1494), in his time the best-paid pain-ter, Lanceloot Blondeel (d.1561) and Pieter Pourbus (d.1584). Their graves and the cemetery may have disap-peared, but their artists' souls still hover in the air.

Walk around the church and turn into Sint-Gilliskoorstraat.

Although the workmen's dwellings in these streets are rather small, they nevertheless display a bricked up win-dow. As it happened, a tax on windows was levied in 1800. As a consequence, a large number of windows were wal-led up.

Woensdagmarkt

**20**

## BRUGES AND THE SEA

For centuries, Potterierei ensured the city's wealth. This canal ran to Damme where it was connected to a large lock, called 'Speie', which in turn was connected to the Zwin, a deep sea channel and tidal inlet. While Damme developed into an outport, Bruges grew into Northwestern Europe's greatest business centre of the Middle Ages. The arts flourished, culture thrived, prosperity seemed to be set for all eternity. The tide turned when Mary of Burgundy suddenly passed away. The relations between Bruges and the Burgundians turned sour and the Burgundian court left the city. The foreign merchants and their wealth followed in its wake. The Zwin silted up and Bruges lost her privileged commercial position. As a result, and compounded by a series of political intrigues, the city fell into a deep winter sleep.

# From Potterierei to the vesten (ramparts)

Turn left into Langerei at the end of the street. Cross the lovely Snaggaard-brug, the first bridge you get to, into Potterierei. Turn left. (You will have to follow the canal for some time.)

After a fair distance along Potterierei is Bruges' Major Seminary (number 72) **05** on your right. A unique place with a lush orchard and meadows with cows at pasture. Between 1628 and 1642 a new Cistercian Abbey (the Dune Abbey) was erected here, which later on would achieve great fame for the wealth and erudition of its occupants. During the French Revolution, the abbey was brought under public ownership, and the abbot and monks were chased away. The 17th-century abbey buildings were first used as a military hospital and then as a military depot and a grammar school before they were eventually taken over by the Major Seminary in 1833. Up to the present day the

Seminary has been training Catholic priests here. Just a few yards further down at number 79B is Our Lady of the Pottery) **16** **35**. Its history goes back to the 13th century. Diligent nuns used to treat pilgrims, travellers and the sick here. From the 15th century onwards, it

**05**

also became a home for the care of the elderly. The Gothic church with its Baroque interior and its rich collection of works of art, accumulated by the hospital throughout the centuries, is a hidden gem that is certainly well worth a visit!

Carry on to the lock and turn right. This idyllic spot is where the canal Damse Vaart heads out across the other side of the ring road towards the equally romantic town of Damme. It's hard to believe that this area around the canal was once a scene of great controversy. Up until the Eighty Years' War, Bruges was connected to Sluis by way of Damme. Ambitious Napoleon Bonaparte had the link with the tidal inlet of the Zwin, the natural predecessor of the Damse Vaart, dredged by Spanish prisoners of war so as to create a watercourse that would run all the way to Antwerp. His plan then was to develop the port city of Antwerp into a naval base, which would enable him to avoid the English sea blockade.

TIP

Have we made you curious? Or do you just like to do things the easy way? If so, leave your bike and car at home and 'all aboard' for a voyage on the Lamme Goedzak 🚢, the most stylish way to reach the town of Damme. Step back in time during this nostalgic journey.
*(For more information see page 65)*

Napoleon's project left Damme cut in twain. The wild plans of the little general were never carried out in full, and by 1815 Napoleon's role in Flanders had come to an end. However, the Dutch King William I also saw the 'benefits' of a connecting canal, and so excavation work was continued until 1824. Belgian independence (1830) meant that the project was finally terminated, by which time it had reached as far as Sluis. Today the low-traffic bicycle path skirting the canal is a most attractive route linking

Sasplein

## THE ARCHERS' GUILD: 120 MEN AND 2 QUEENS!

Although this used to be one of the poorer areas of the city for a very long time, the district includes two exclusive clubs. A greater contradiction cannot be found! Are you sitting comfortably out of harm's way on the slope of Sint-Jans-huis Mill? Then look down on your left. There is Saint George's Guild **40**, a fellowship of crossbow men. Down on your right is Saint Sebastian's Guild **41** with its remarkably elegant tower. This guild goes back more than six centuries, which makes it unique in the world. The society numbers 120 male members exactly and two notable female honorary members: the Belgian queen Mathilde and the British queen. Ever since the exiled English king Charles II took up residence in Bruges in the 17th century, the city and the British Royal Family have always been closely associated. Whenever the British Royal Family is on a state visit to Belgium, so the rumour goes, they first of all pop in at the Saint Sebastian's Archers' Guild.

Bruges with Damme. The trip is highly recommended, as it traverses le plat pays, that flat country made famous by Jacques Brel in the moving song of that name. Imagine! In the middle of a unique polder landscape this truly poetic canal strip, bordered by lofty poplars bended down by eternal westerly winds.

Turn right and carry on along the Vesten (canals), which surround the city like a ring of green.
In the 16th century, more than thirty windmills were turning their sails here. Today only four are left. In the 18th century, the millers stood by helplessly when bread consumption took a dive and people started to consume more potatoes. Eventually steam machines would take over the millers' tasks. The Koelewei Mill **31** and Sint-Janshuis Mill **39** are open to visitors. The miller will happily explain the workings of his mill, and he will gladly give a milling demonstration, too. Make sure you climb the slopes on which the Sint-Janshuis Mill and the Bonne Chiere Mill (just next to the Kruispoort/Cross Gate **12**) proudly stand! The hills afford a fantastic panoramic view of the city. This is the perfect spot to brush up on your amassed knowledge of Bruges.

And there's more! Down below on your right is Verloren Hoek (the Lost Corner), now an authentic working-class district, but back in the 19th century an impoverished neighbourhood with such a bad reputation that even the police didn't dare enter its streets.

## Silent Bruges

Descend down the slope and turn right into Rolweg.

---

TIP

Interested in a little something 'extra'? Then go and take a look at the Albrecht Rodenbachstraat, another of the city's hidden gems. This green suburb *avant la lettre* offers an almost unbroken succession of step-gables and other fascinating facades, each fronted by a delightful little garden.

---

Right on the corner is the Gezelle Museum **24**, the birthplace of Guido Gezelle (1830-1899), one of Flanders' most venerable poets. On display are handwritten letters, writing material and a deliciously peaceful garden with an age-old Corsican pine. Gezelle's parents worked here as gardener and caretaker, in exchange for which they and their family received free board and lodging. Little Guido grew up in these idyllic surroundings. He would eventually return to Bruges many years later and after many a peregrination. Upon his return he became curate of Saint Walburga's Church **24**. He also took over the running of the English Convent **04** (Carmersstraat 83-85), where he would die. These were his last words, reportedly: 'I have so loved hearing the birds singing.' Here, in this most verdant part of Bruges, we still know precisely what the priest and poet meant.

Turn into Balstraat, the second street on the left.

This picturesque working-man's alley houses the Folklore Museum (Volkskundemuseum) **45**. The 17th-century row of single-room dwellings, restored and converted into authentic artisans' interiors such as a milliner's, a confectioner's and a small classroom, will take you back to bygone days.

The tower of the 15th-century Jerusalem Chapel **08** can easily be spotted from these premises. This chapel was commissioned by the Adornes, a prominent Bruges merchant family of Genovese origin, who lived in a magnificent mansion **28** on the Peperstraat. In 1470 Anselm Adornes collected one of his sons (the father had no fewer

> **TIP**
>
> If you feel like taking a break, you are welcome to rest your tired feet in the large, walled garden of the Folklore Museum. It is a delightful oasis of calm in the heart of the city, and even has its own outdoor pétanque alley!

than sixteen children) in Padua to set off on a pilgrimage to the Holy Land. Upon his return to Bruges, Anselm decided to build an exact copy of the Church of the Holy Sepulchre. The result was remarkable.

On the corner, at Balstraat 16, you can visit the new Lace Centre **30**, which has been installed in the fully

renovated old lace School. If you visit during one of the many lace demonstrations (2.00-5.00 p.m.), it is almost like stepping back in time.

At the crossroads turn right into Jeruzalemstraat; then, at the church, left unto Sint-Annaplein.

The tiny square is dominated by the apparently simple Church of Saint Anne **19**. Its exterior may be austere, but its interior is one of Bruges' most splendid examples of Baroque architecture. The restoration work of recent times has now been completed, so feel free to pop inside and take a look at its many treasures. As this neighbourhood gradually became more prestigious, the church did the same!

With the church behind you turn left into Sint-Annakerkstraat and then right into Sint-Annarei.

At the corner of the confluence of the two waterways one of Bruges' most handsome town houses is proudly showing off its Rococo credentials (Sint-Annarei no. 22). Sit yourself down on a shady bench and enjoy this exceptional prospect.

Retrace your steps for just a few yards and turn left into Blekersstraat next to the bridge.

Café Vlissinghe at number 2 is undoubtedly Bruges' oldest café. This has been a tavern since 1515. It is no surprise then that you will find oodles of ambiance here. It is therefore the perfect place to settle down and let the wonderful memories of your walk slowly sink in. A local beer will be your ideal companion. Cheers!

Church of Our Lady

# Know your way around **Bruges**

Triennial of Contemporary Art and Architecture, Bruges 2015

# Exploring Bruges

You might want to stroll, amble and saunter down the streets of Bruges all day long. However, why not try to see the city from a different perspective? During a walking or bicycle tour, a guide will show you numerous secret places. Maybe you would prefer a boat trip on the mysterious canals – an unforgettable experience! And a ride in a horse-drawn carriage must surely be the perfect romantic outing. Sport-lovers can even do a guided run around the city. Or perhaps you simply want to tour all the highlights as quickly and as comfortably as possible? Then a minibus with expert commentary is what you need. And what about a balloon ride or a daytrip on a Vespa, or an electric Segway? The choice is yours!

### 🔲 🚤 Bruges by boat

A visit to Bruges isn't complete without a boat trip on its canals. Go aboard at any of the five landing stages (consult city map) for a half-hour trip that allows you to appreciate the most noteworthy delights of the city from a completely different angle.

OPEN > March to mid-November, daily, 10.00 a.m.-6.00 p.m. (last departure at 5.30 p.m.)

PRICE > € 8.00; children aged 4 to 11 (accompanied by an adult): € 4.00; children under 4: free; Brugge City Card (during the period 1/3 to 15/11): free

### 🔲 🚂 Lamme Goedzak (steam wheeler) Damme

The nostalgic river boat 'Lamme Goedzak', with room for 170 passengers, sails back and forth between the Noorweegse Kaai (Norwegian Quay) in Bruges and the centre of Damme, the town of the legendary character Tijl Uilenspiegel (Owlglass), whose friend was called ... Lamme Goedzak!

OPEN > During the period 1/4 to 30/9: departures from Bruges to Damme, daily at 10.00 a.m., 12.00 a.m., 2.00 p.m.

and 4.00 p.m.; departures from Damme to Bruges, daily at 11.00 a.m., 1.00 p.m., 3.00 p.m. and 5.20 p.m.

PRICE > € 7.50 (one-way ticket) or € 10.50 (return ticket); 65+: € 7.00 (one-way ticket) or € 9.50 (return ticket); children aged 3 to 11: € 6.00 (one-way ticket) or € 8.50 (return ticket); Brugge City Card: € 8.00 (return ticket)

INFORMATION > Tel. +32 (0)50 28 86 10, www.bootdamme-brugge.be; public transport: bus no. 4 or no. 14, stop: Sasplein near the Dampoort (Damme Gate); from there it is a 5-10 minute walk to the landing stage at the Noorweegse Kaai 31 (Norwegian Quay – City map: J1).

### 🔲 Port Cruise Zeebrugge

The port cruise departs from the old fishing port on board of the 'Zephira', a passenger ship. The tour takes in the naval base, the Pierre Vandamme Lock (one of the largest locks in the world), the gas terminal, the wind turbine park, the 'tern' island, the cruise ships and the dredging vessels. You will also see how the massive container ships are unloaded at the quay. Each visitor is given an easy-to-use

audio-visual guide in the desired language. You can also download the information on your smart phone. An experience that offers a unique insight into the port and its manifold activities.

OPEN > During the period 1/4 until 14/10: weekends and public holidays at 2.00 p.m.; during the period 1/7 until 31/8, daily at 2.00 p.m. and 4.00 p.m; during the period 1/8 until 17/8: daily extra round trip at 11.00 a.m.

PRICE > € 9.50; 60+: € 9.00; children aged 3 to 11: € 7.00; Brugge City Card: € 7.00

INFORMATION > Embarkation at Jacques Brelsteiger, Tijdokstraat (Old Fishing Port), Zeebrugge, tel. 32 (0)59 70 62 94, www.franlis.be; public transport: train Bruges-Zeebrugge, from the station Zeebrugge-Dorp: about 15 to 20 minutes on foot or from the station Zeebrugge-Strand: coast tram (direction: Knokke), to tram stop: Zeebrugge-Kerk (church)

## Bruges on foot

Not exhausted from walking around yet? Are you still in the mood for a guided tour? Then hurry to the tourist office at 't Zand (Concertgebouw) and regis-

ter for a two-hour fascinating guided walk. Languages: English, Dutch and French

OPEN > January/February/March/November/December : Monday, Wednesday and Saturday at 4.00 p.m. and Sunday at 10.30 a.m.

April: Saturday at 2.30 p.m. and Sunday at 10.30 a.m., but during the Easter holidays (6/4 to 19/4) daily.

May/June/September/October: Saturday at 2.30 p.m. and Sunday at 10.30 a.m.

July/August and during the period 6/4 to 19/4: Monday to Saturday at 2.30 p.m. and Sunday at 10.30 a.m.

On 5/4 (Easter Sunday), 6/4 (Easter Monday), 15/5 (the Friday after Ascension Day) at 2.30 p.m.; 24/5 (Whit Sunday), 21/7 (National Holiday), 15/8 (Assumption of Mary), 1/11 (All Saints' Day) and 11/11 (Armistice Day) at 10.30 a.m. There is no walk on 14/5 (Ascension Day).

PRICE > € 12.50; children under 12: free; Brugge City Card (during the period 1/11 to 31/3): free

TICKETS > Tourist office at the Markt (Historium) and 't Zand (Concertgebouw) or www.ticketsbrugge.be

## Photo Tour Brugge

Whether you are a photography expert or a photography novice, during the Photo Tour Andy McSweeney will take you to all the most photogenic spots in town! What are the 'must-have' shots for the photo-reportage of your city trip to Bruges? You will learn this and lots more beside during a fascinating two-hour walk, complete with dozens of practical photography tips from Andy. The rendezvous point is the Basilica of the Holy Blood on the Burg Square. The walks are given in English, but Dutch and/or French can also be arranged on request.

*(Read more about Andy in the interview on page 112)*

*(Read more about Andy in the interview on page 112)*

OPEN > Four walks are organized each day, each with a different theme: 'Edges of Brugge' (at 10.00 a.m.) focuses on the side streets and canals; 'Essential Brugge' (1.00 p.m.) zooms in on the toppers; during 'Hidden Brugge' (4.00 p.m.) you will go in search of some of the city's less well-known corners and at 8.00 p.m. you can experience 'Bruges by Night'.

PRICE > € 50.00. Every paying participant receives five Bruges photos, specially taken by Andy McSweeney; every participating photographer can bring along one other non-photographer free of charge. Maximum of 5 photographers per walk. Prior reservation is recommended.

INFORMATION > Tel. +32 (0)486 17 52 75, info@phototourbrugge.com, www.phototourbrugge.com

## Running around Bruges

**Tourist Run Brugge – guided tours**
Accompanied by a guide you run – at a gentle pace – through the streets and alleyways of Bruges. Because you either run early in the morning or early in the evening, you can freely admire Bruges. The circuit is 9.5 km long. With the explanation that you receive along the way, you should allow 1 to 1.5 hours for completion. The start and finish points are both on the Market Square, at the foot of the statue of Jan Breydel and Pieter de Coninck. On prior request, you will be picked up at your hotel or from wherever you are staying.

OPEN > Monday to Sunday at 7.00 a.m., 8.00 a.m., 9.00 a.m., 5.00 p.m., 6 p.m., 7 p.m., 8 p.m. or 9 p.m. Prior reservation is necessary.

PRICE > € 15.00

INFORMATION > Tel. +32 (0)473 88 37 17, info@touristrunbrugge.be, www.touristrunbrugge.be

## 🐎 Bruges by horse-drawn carriage

The half-hour carriage ride along Bruges' historic winding streets trots off on

the Markt (at the Burg on Wednesday morning). Halfway through the ride the carriage briefly stops at the Beguinage. The coachman gives expert commentary en route.

OPEN > Daily, 9.00 a.m.-6.00 p.m.; July and August, 9.00 a.m.-10.00 p.m.

PRICE > € 44.00 per carriage; a carriage seats up to 5 people

INFORMATION > www.hippo.be/koets

## Bruges by hot air balloon

### Bruges Ballooning

The most adventurous and probably the most romantic way to discover Bruges is by hot-air balloon. Bruges Ballooning organizes both a morning flight (including a champagne breakfast) and an evening flight (including a bite to eat, champagne or a beer) over Bruges. The whole trip lasts for three hours, with at least one hour in the air. You will be collected from wherever you are staying.

OPEN > During the period 1/4 to 31/10: daily flights, but only if booked in advance; bookings can be made on the day itself with a few hours' notice, providing there are no prior reservations.

PRICE > € 180.00; children aged 4 to 12: € 100.00; Brugge City Card: € 135.00

INFORMATION > Tel. +32 (0)475 97 28 87, info@bruges-ballooning.com, www.bruges-ballooning.com

## Bruges by bus

### City Tour Bruges

The mini buses of City Tour provide a guided tour that passes all the most beautiful spots in the city. Every half hour, they depart from the Markt (Market Square) for a 50 minute drive along the most important highlights of the town. Individual headphones provide an explanation in 16 different languages.

OPEN > Daily (also on Sunday and public holidays). The first bus leaves at 10.00 a.m. During the period 1/9 to 31/5, there are tours until sunset; during

the period 1/6 to 31/8 the last bus ride leaves at 7.00 p.m.

**PRICE >** € 16.00; children aged 6 to 11: € 9.50; children under 6: free.

**INFORMATION >** Tel. +32 (0) 50 35 50 24 (Monday to Friday, 10.00 a.m-12.00 p.m.) or info@citytour.be, www.citytour.be

## Bruges by bike

**QuasiMundo Biketours Bruges**

• 'Bruges By Bike' > The narrow streets reveal the medieval character of the ancient port. The guide's fascinating stories will catapult you back to a time when knights and counts ruled the town. It goes without saying that there is a stop along the way for a thirst-quenching Belgian beer.

**OPEN >** During the period 1/3 to 15/11: daily, 10.00 a.m.-12.30 p.m.

• 'The Hinterland of Bruges by bike' > A tour through Bruges' wet- and woodlands, passing through medieval towns such as Damme, peaceful Flemish agrarian villages and dead straight canals. A must-see for anyone who loves the peaceful greenery of the countryside.

**OPEN >** During the period 1/3 to 15/11: daily, 1.00 p.m.-5.00 p.m.

Meeting Point: at the entrance of the Town Hall on the Burg, ten minutes before tour departure. English spoken. Booking is required.

**PRICE >** Including bike, guide, raincoat and refreshment in a local café: € 28.00; youngsters aged 14 to 26: € 26.00; children under 14: free. If you bring your own bike you get a reduction:

adults: € 17.00; youngsters aged 14 to 26: € 16.00

**INFORMATION >** Tel. +32 (0)50 33 07 75, info@quasimundo.eu, www.quasimundo.eu

**The Pink Bear Bike Tours**

A mere five minutes away from bustling Bruges lies one of the prettiest rural areas in Europe. You ride to historic Damme, the handsome medieval market town, once Bruges' outport. Furthermore, a guide will show you the most enchanting places of the Polders. It goes without saying that there is also a stop at a pleasant café for some Belgian Beers and/or Belgian waffles. On your return you follow the beautiful poplar planted banks of a canal and discover some of Bruges' best-kept secrets. Meeting Point: Belfry. English spoken.

**OPEN >** Daily, 10.25 a.m.-2.00 p.m. Booking is recommended; in January

*Addresses of locations where you can hire bikes are given in the section 'Practical information' on page 13-14.*

and February only possible with prior reservation.

PRICE > € 25.00; youngsters aged 9 to 26: € 23.00; children under 9: free; € 18.00 if you bring your own bike.

INFORMATION > Tel. +32 (0)50 61 66 86, pinkbear@telenet.be, www.pinkbear.freeservers.com

### The Green Bike Tour

A guided trip to the polders, the flat countryside around Bruges. The tour pulls up at medieval Damme and other important sights along the way for a little extra commentary. Tandem rides can also be booked. Meeting point: 't Zand, Concertgebouw. English, Dutch and French spoken. Booking is required.

OPEN > Daily, by appointment only

PRICE > € 15.00 (bike); € 30.00 (tandem); € 9.00 if you bring your own bike.

INFORMATION > Tel. +32 (0)50 61 26 67, arlando@telenet.be

### Bruges on a Segway

Moment

If you want to discover Bruges in an original manner, why not choose a Segway tour? A Segway is a self-stabilising electric vehicle with two wheels that you operate while standing on it in an upright position. In addition to the city tour, which takes you to the historic sites and the most magnificent monuments and buildings in Bruges, you can also opt for the chocolate tour, the Segway-horse tram tour, the brewery tour (with a visit to the Halve Maan Brewery) or an

evening tour in which you combine a ride through the beautifully illuminated inner city with a three-course menu.

OPEN > Daily, except on Wednesday: guided tour at 10.00 a.m., 12.00 p.m., 2.00 p.m. and 4.00 p.m.; on Saturday also at 6.00 p.m. (on Monday: no ride at 10.00 a.m.). Thematic tours on request. Booking is strongly recommended: a minimum of 2 and maximum of 20 people per tour. Closed 1/1, during the periods 12/1 to 11/2, 19/8 to 26/8 and 25/12.

PRICE > Guide included, 1 hour: € 35.00, 2 hours: € 50.00. The tour languages are Dutch, French, English and German.

INFORMATION > Tel. +32 (0)50 68 87 70 or +32 (0)495 90 60 60, info@segway-brugge.be, www.segwaybrugge.be

## Bruges by motorbike

### 🏍 Electric Scooters

For anyone who wants to discover Bruges quickly, silently and in an ecologically friendly way by scooter.

OPEN > During the period 1/4 to 30/9: Tuesday to Sunday, 10.00 a.m.- 6.00 p.m.; during the period 1/10 to 31/3: Tuesday to Saturday, 1.00 p.m.- 6.00 p.m. (also possible from 10.00 a.m. by appointment or with a reservation)

PRICE > Including helmet and insurance. For an A-class scooter (max. speed 25 kph)> Emoto 87, for 2 persons: 2 hours: € 35.00; 4 hours: € 50.00; 8 hours: € 65.00 (Brugge City Card: € 48.75). For a B-class scooter (max. speed 45 kph)> E-max 110S, for 2 persons: 2 hours: € 40.00; 8 hours: € 75.00 (Brugge City Card: € 56.25).
For an electric bike > 2 hours: € 10.00, 4 hours: € 18.00 and 8 hours: 30.00

CONDITIONS > Minimum age of driver: 23 years; for a B-class scooter: A3 or B category driving license; deposit of € 100.00 to be paid before departure.

INFORMATION > Gentpoortstraat 62, tel. +32 (0)474 09 19 18, info@electric-scooters.be, www.electric-scooters.be

### Vespa tours

Discover Bruges' Hinterland in style: book a guided tour with a snazzy Vespa scooter and traverse the green polders, authentic villages and breath-taking landscapes. A couple of surprises are provided en route. Half-day and day tours. You can also opt for the Cook & Drive a Vespa arrangement, a daylong programme with a fun mix of cooking and sightseeing. Booking is required. Meeting point: 't Zand. Dutch, French and English spoken. If you prefer to explore the city unaccompanied, you can also hire a Vespa.

OPEN > During the period 1/3 to 15/11: daily, 9.30 a.m.-6.00 p.m.

PRICE > Including helmet, experienced guide and insurance: half day tour: 1 person per Vespa: € 65.00; 2 persons per Vespa: € 80.00; day tour: 1 person per Vespa: € 100.00; 2 persons per Vespa: € 115.00. Hiring a Vespa without guide, with helmets and insurance included: half day tour: 1 person per Vespa: € 50.00; 2 persons per Vespa: € 70.00.

CONDITIONS > Minimum age of driver: 21 years, driving licence B, deposit of € 200.00 to be paid before departure.

INFORMATION > Tel. +32 (0)497 64 86 48, bdpvespatours@gmail.com, www.vespatours-brugge.be

# Museums, places of interest and attractions

Some places are so special, so breathtaking or so unique that you simply have to see them. Bruges is filled to the brim with wonderful witnesses of a prosperous past. Although the Flemish primitives are undoubtedly Bruges' showpiece attraction, museum devotees in search of much more will not be disappointed. Indeed, the Bruges range of attractions is truly magnificent. From modern plastic art by way of Michelangelo's world-famous *Madonna and Child* to the brand new Lace Centre. It's all there for you to discover! With the Bruges City Card, you can visit numerous museums, places of interest and attractions for free ▦ or with a good discount ▦.

## 🏛️♿ 01 Archeologiemuseum (Archaeological Museum)

This museum presents the unwritten history of Bruges. Its motto: feel your past beneath your feet. Discover the history of the city through different kinds of search and hands-on activities. A fascinating mix of archaeological finds, riddles, replicas and reconstructions shed light on daily life in times gone by, from the home to the workplace and from birth till death.

OPEN > Tuesday to Sunday, 9.30 a.m.-12.30 p.m. and 1.30 p.m.-5.00 p.m.; last admission: 12.00 p.m. and 4.30 p.m. (open on Easter Monday and Whit Monday)

ADDITIONAL CLOSING DATES >

1/1, 14/5 (1.00 p.m.-5.00 p.m.) and 25/12

PRICE > € 4.00; 65+ and youngsters aged 12 to 25: € 3.00; children under 12: free; Brugge City Card: free

INFORMATION > Mariastraat 36A, tel. +32 (0)50 44 87 43, www.museabrugge.be

## 🏛️ 02 Arentshuis

In this elegant 18th-century town house with its picturesque garden the work of the versatile British artist Frank Brangwyn (1867-1956) is on display on the top floor. Brangwyn was both a graphic artist and a painter, as well as a designer of carpets, furniture and ceramics. The ground floor is the setting for temporary plastic art exhibitions.

OPEN > Tuesday to Sunday, 9.30 a.m.-5.00 p.m.; last admission: 4.30 p.m. (open on Easter Monday and Whit Monday)

ADDITIONAL CLOSING DATES >

1/1, 14/5 (1.00 p.m.-5.00 p.m.) and 25/12

PRICE > € 4.00; 65+ and youngsters aged 12 to 25: € 3.00; children under 12: free; Brugge City Card: free; combination ticket with Groeninge Museum possible *(See page 91)*

INFORMATION > Dijver 16, www.museabrugge.be

## 🏛️♿ 01

## Basiliek van het Heilig Bloed (Basilica of the Holy Blood)

The double church, dedicated to Our Lady and Saint Basil in the 12th century and a basilica since 1923, consists of a lower church that has maintained its Romanesque character and a neo-Gothic upper church, in which the relic

of the Holy Blood is preserved. The renovated treasury, with numerous valuable works of art, is also worth a visit.

**OPEN >** Daily, 9.30 a.m.-12.00 p.m. and 2.00 p.m.-5.00 p.m.; during the period 15/11 to 31/3 closed on Wednesday afternoon

**PRICE >** Double church: free; treasury: € 2.00; children under 13: free, Brugge City Card: free

**INFORMATION >** Burg 13, tel. +32 (0)50 33 67 92, www.holyblood.com

## 02 02 03 Begijnhof (Beguinage)

The 'Princely Beguinage Ten Wijngaarde' with its white-coloured house fronts, tranquil convent garden and beguinage museum was founded in 1245. Nowadays, this item of World Heritage is inhabited by the sisters of the Order of Saint Benedict. The Beguinage entrance gate closes without fail at 6.30 p.m.

**OPEN >** Beguinage: daily, 6.30 a.m.-6.30 p.m.; Beguine's house: Monday to Saturday, 10.00 a.m.-5.00 p.m., Sunday 2.00 p.m.-5.00 p.m.

**PRICE >** Beguinage: free; Beguine's house: € 2.00; 65+: € 1.50; children aged 8 to 11 and students (on display of a valid student card): € 1.00; Brugge City Card: free

**INFORMATION >** Begijnhof 24-28-30, tel. +32 (0)50 33 00 11, www.monasteria.org, www.bezinningshuizen.be

## 10 04 Belfort (Belfry)

The most important of Bruges' towers stands 83 metres tall. It houses, amongst other things, a carillon with 47 melodious bells. In the reception area, waiting visitors can discover all kinds of interesting information about the history and working of this unique world-heritage protected belfry. Those who take on the challenge of climbing the tower can pause for a breather on the way up in the old treasury, where the city's charters, seal and public funds were kept during the Middle Ages, and

## Boudewijn Seapark Bruges

Welcome to the Boudewijn Seapark, where dolphins steal the show with their spectacular leaps and where sea lions and seals perform the craziest tricks. But it is not only the sea mammals in this family park that will charm you, but also the 20 outdoor park attractions that offer guaranteed fun for young and old alike. Finally, *Bobo's Indoor* has 12 great indoor attractions, as well as Bobo's Aqua Splash, providing 1,100 square meters of wonderful water fun.

OPEN > During the 'summer period' (4/4 to 27/9) the amusement park, shows and Bobo's Indoor are open: during the Easter holidays (4/4 to 19/4) and weekends in April: 10.00 a.m.-5.00 p.m.; in May and June: daily, except Wednesday, 10.00 a.m.-5.00 p.m.; July and August: daily, 10.00 a.m.-6.00 p.m.; September: only on weekends, 10.00 a.m.-6.00 p.m.

During the 'winter period' (30/09 to 31/3) only Bobo's Indoor and the dolphin shows are open to the public: on Wednesday, Saturday and Sunday:

also at the level of the impressive clock or in the carillonneur's chamber. Finally, after a tiring 366 steps, your efforts will be rewarded with a breath-taking and unforgettable panoramic view of Bruges and her surroundings.

OPEN > Daily, 9.30 a.m.-5.00 p.m.; last admission: 4.15 p.m. Due to security reasons only 70 visitors are allowed at a time. It is impossible to make prior reservations for your visit. Each visitor has to wait in line. Please consider a certain waiting period.

ADDITIONAL CLOSING DATES >
1/1, 14/5 (1.00 p.m.-5.00 p.m.) and 25/12
PRICE > € 8.00; 65+ and youngsters aged 6 to 25: € 6.00; children under 6: free; Brugge City Card: free
INFORMATION > Markt 7, tel. +32 (0)50 44 87 43, www.museabrugge.be

2.00 p.m.-6.00 p.m. and during (Belgian) school holidays, 10.00- 6.00 p.m. During the Christmas vacation (21/12 to 3/1/16) you can visit the Nocturne Aqua Show in the dolphinarium.

ADDITIONAL CLOSING DATES >
1/1, 24/12, 25/12 and 31/12

PRICE > All-inclusive ticket for the 'summer period': adults older than 12 years: € 25.00; children taller than 1 metre and younger than 12: € 21.00; children between 85 and 99 centimetres: € 8.00. 'Winter period': different combination tickets with the dolphinarium, everyone taller than 85 cm: € 19.00; Pay&Display car park ('summer period'): € 7.00; Brugge City Card: € 16.00

INFO EN TICKETS > A. De Baeckestraat 12, St.-Michiels, tel. +32 (0)50 38 38 38, www.boudewijnseapark.be. Tickets at the amusement park entrance or at the tourist office 🛈 't Zand (Concertgebouw). Boudewijn Sea Park is situated just outside the city centre and is connected to the Bicycle Route Network; public transport: bus no. 7 or no. 17 - stop: 'Boudewijnpark'

### 🏠 ⑪ Brouwerij 'De Halve Maan' (Brewery)

The 'Halve Maan' (Half Moon) is an authentic and historic brewery in the centre of Bruges. This 'home' brewery is a family business with a tradition stretching back through six generations to 1856. This is where the Bruges city beer – the 'Brugse Zot' – is brewed: a strong-tasting, high-fermentation beer based on malt, hops and special yeast. There are guided tours of the brewery every day in a number of different languages. After the tour, visitors are treated to the blond version of the 'Brugse Zot'. If you want to take a souvenir back home with you, why not pay a visit to the museum shop?

OPEN > During the period 1/4 to 31/10: daily, 11.00 a.m.-4.00 p.m. (Saturday till 5.00 p.m.), guided tours every hour; during the period 1/11 to 31/3: Monday to Friday, guided tour at 11.00 a.m. & 3.00 p.m.; Saturday 11.00 a.m.-5.00 p.m. and Sunday 11.00 a.m.-4.00 p.m., guided tours every hour. Consult the website for possible changes in the opening hours.

ADDITIONAL CLOSING DATES > 1/1, 5/1 to 9/1, 12/1 to 16/1, 19/1 to 23/1, 26/1 to 30/1, 24/12 and 25/12

PRICE > Including refreshment: € 8.50; children aged 6 to 12: € 4.25; children under 6: free; Brugge City Card: free
INFORMATION > Walplein 26, tel. +32 (0)50 44 42 22, www.halvemaan.be

## ⑬ Bruges Beer Museum

The Bruges Beer Museum has recently been opened on the upper floors of the old post office on the Market Square. It tells you the story of beer in a fun and innovative way. With a mini iPad as your guide, you will discover all the most fascinating features of beer (and that includes tasting!). Immerse yourself in the beer history of Belgium and of Bruges. Discover the many different types of beer and unravel the mysteries of the brewery process. The kids' tour tells the same story, but specially adapted for children (5 to 15 years old).
OPEN > Daily, 10.00 a.m.-6.30 p.m.; last entrance at 5.00 p.m.
ADDITIONAL CLOSING DATES > 1/1, 25/12
PRICE > Including iPad (with headphones) and 3 beer samples: € 11.00; including iPad (with headphones) but without beer samples: € 7.00; children

aged 5 to 15 (kids tour): € 6.00; children under 5: free.
INFORMATION > Breidelstraat 3 (Post Office), tel. +32 (0)479 35 95 67, www.brugesbeermuseum.com

## 🏙 ♿ 01 03 08 ⑭ Brugse Vrije (Liberty of Bruges)

From this mansion, erected between 1722 and 1727, Bruges' rural surroundings were governed. The building functioned as a court of justice between 1795 and 1984. Today the city archives are stored here. They safeguard Bruges' written memory. The premises also boast an old assize court and a renaissance hall with a monumental 16th-century timber, marble and alabaster fireplace made by Lanceloot Blondeel.
OPEN > Daily, 9.30 a.m.-12.30 p.m. and 1.30 p.m.-5.00 p.m.; last admission: 12.00 p.m. and 4.30 p.m.
ADDITIONAL CLOSING DATES > 1/1, 14/5 (1.00 p.m.-5.00 p.m.) and 25/12
PRICE > Including City Hall visit: € 4.00; 65+ and youngsters aged 12 to 25: € 3.00; children under 12: free; Brugge City Card: free (tickets are sold in the town hall).

INFORMATION > Burg 11A, tel. +32 (0)50 44 87 43, www.museabrugge.be

### 🏛 ⑮ Choco-Story (Chocolate Museum)

The museum dips its visitors in the history of cocoa and chocolate. From the Maya and the Spanish conquistadores to the chocolate connoisseurs of today. A chocolate hunt gives children the chance to discover the museum. Chocolates are made by hand and sampled on the premises.

OPEN > During the period 1/9 to 30/6: daily, 10.00 a.m.-5.00 p.m.; last admission: 4.15 p.m.; in July and August: daily, 10.00 a.m.-6.00 p.m.; last admission: 5.15 p.m.

ADDITIONAL CLOSING DATES > 1/1, 5/1 to 16/1, 24/12, 25/12 and 31/12

PRICE > € 8.00; 65+ and students: € 7.00; children aged 6 to 11: € 5.00; children under 6: free; Brugge City Card: free; several combination tickets possible *(See page 91)*

INFORMATION > Wijnzakstraat 2,tel. +32 (0)50 61 22 37, www.choco-story.be

### Cozmix volkssterrenwacht (Public Observatory) Beisbroek

In the Cozmix observatory you will be able to admire the beauty of the sun, moon and planets in glorious close-up, thanks to the powerful telescope. In the planetarium more than 7,000 stars are projected onto the interior of the dome. Spectacular video images take you on a journey through the mysteries of the universe: you will fly over the surface of Mars and pass through the rings of Saturn. The artistic planet-pathway (with sculptures by Jef Claerhout) will complete your voyage of discovery into outer space.

OPEN > Wednesday and Sunday, 2.30 p.m.–6.00 p.m., Friday, 8.00 p.m.-10.00 p.m.; planetarium shows on Wednesday at 3.00 p.m., on Friday at 8.30 p.m. and on Sunday at 3.00 p.m. and 4.30 p.m. During (Belgian) school holidays there are extra shows on Monday, Tuesday and Thursday at 3.00 p.m. There are shows in languages other than Dutch (one week in French, the other week in English) on Wednesday at 4.30 p.m.

ADDITIONAL CLOSING DATES > 1/1, 25/12
PRICE > € 5.00; youngsters aged 5 to 17 :
€ 4.00
INFORMATION > Zeeweg 96, Sint-Andries, tel. +32 (0)50 39 05 66, www.cozmix.be; public transport: bus no. 52 or no. 55 - stop: Varsenare, Zeeweg

## 🏛 ⑰ Museum-Gallery Xpo Salvador Dalí

In the Belfry, you can admire a fantastic collection of world-famous graphics and statues by the great artist Dalí. They are all authentic works of art that are described in the Catalogues Raisonnés, which details Salvador Dalí's oeuvre. An audio-guide (Dutch, French or English) leads you through the collection, which is presented in a sensational Daliesque décor of mirrors and shocking pink.
OPEN > Daily, 10.00 a.m.-6.00 p.m.
ADDITIONAL CLOSING DATES > 1/1, 25/12
PRICE > € 10.00; 65+ and students: € 8.00; children under 12: free; audio-guide (available in 3 languages): € 2.00; Brugge City Card: free; several combination tickets possible
*(See page 91)*

*(See page 91)*

INFORMATION > Markt 7, tel. +32 (0)50 33 83 44, www.dali-interart.be

## 🏛 ⑳ Diamantmuseum Brugge (Bruges Diamond Museum)

Did you know that the technique of cutting diamonds was first applied in Bruges more than 500 years ago? The Bruges Diamond Museum tells this story in a series of fascinating exhibition displays. And there is a live demonstration of diamond cutting each day – a memorable experience, not to be missed! You can also take a look inside the original diamond workshop and shop of a renowned Brussels jeweller. In the diamond laboratory, microscopes and other equipment allow visitors, both young and old alike, to discover the true beauty of diamonds – now one of Belgium's leading export products! – in all their many forms.
OPEN > Daily, 10.30 a.m.-5.30 p.m.
All year round there is a diamond-cutting demonstration at 12.15 p.m. each day; during the weekends, (Belgian) school holidays and the period 1/4 to 31/10 there is an extra demonstration at

3.15 p.m. (visitors need to be present 15 minutes in advance).

ADDITIONAL CLOSING DATES >
1/1, 5/1 to 23/1 and 25/12

PRICE > Museum: € 8.00, museum + diamond-cutting demo: € 11.00; children aged 6 to 12, students (on display of a valid student card) and 65+: museum: € 7.00, museum +diamond-cutting demo: € 10.00; children under 6: free; Brugge City Card: free; a combination ticket is possible *(See page 91)*

INFORMATION > Katelijnestraat 43, tel. +32 (0)50 34 20 56, www.diamondmuseum.be

## 08 22 Frietmuseum (Belgian Fries Museum)

This didactical museum sketches the history of the potato, Belgian fries and the various sauces and dressings that accompany this most delicious and most famous of Belgian comestibles. The museum is housed in Saaihalle, one of Bruges' most attractive buildings. Show your entrance ticket and enjoy € 0.40 discount on a portion of French fries (in the basement).

OPEN > Daily, 10.00 a.m.-5.00 p.m.; last admission: 4.15 p.m.

ADDITIONAL CLOSING DATES >
1/1, 5/1 to 16/1, 24/12, 25/12 and 31/12

PRICE > € 7.00; 65+ and students: € 6.00; children aged 6 to 11: € 5.00; children under 6: free; Brugge City Card: free; combination ticket possible *(See page 91)*

INFORMATION > Vlamingstraat 33, tel. +32 (0)50 34 01 50, www.frietmuseum.be

## 07 23 Gentpoort (Gate of Ghent)

The Gate of Ghent is one of four remaining medieval city gates. An entrance for foreigners, a border with the outside world for the townspeople of Bruges. The gate was a part of the city's defences as well as a passageway for

the movement of produce and merchandise. Note the statue in the niche above the roadway: this is Saint Adrian, who was believed to protect the city during times of plague. The Ghent Gate is at its most beautiful in the evening, when it is quite literally in the spotlight.

OPEN > Saturday and Sunday, 9.30 a.m.-12.30 p.m. and 1.30 p.m.-5.00 p.m.; last admission: 12.00 p.m. and 4.30 p.m.

PRICE > € 4.00; 65+ and youngsters aged 12 to 25: € 3.00; children under 12: free; Brugge City Card: free

INFORMATION > Gentpoortvest, tel. +32 (0)50 44 87 43, www.museabrugge.be

## 🏛 24 Gezellemuseum (Gezelle Museum)

This literary and biographical museum about the life of Guido Gezelle (1830-

1899), one of Flanders' most famous poets, was established in the house where he was born, situated in a peaceful working-class district of the city. In addition to displays about his life and works, there are also temporary presentations about (literary) art. Next to the house there is a romantic garden, with Jan Fabre's *The Man Who Gives a Light* as the main attraction.

OPEN > Tuesday to Sunday: 9.30 a.m.-12.30 p.m. and 1.30 p.m.-5.00 p.m.; last admission: 12.00 a.m. and 4.30 p.m. (open on Easter Monday and Whit Monday)

ADDITIONAL CLOSING DATES > 1/1, 14/5 (1.00 p.m.-5.00 p.m.) and 25/12

PRICE > € 4.00; 65+ and youngsters aged 12 to 25: € 3.00; children under 12: free; Brugge City Card: free

INFORMATION > Rolweg 64, tel. +32 (0)50 44 87 43, www.museabrugge.be

## 🏛 ♿ 25 Groeningemuseum (Groeninge Museum)

The Groeninge Museum provides a varied overview of the history of Belgian visual art, with as highlight the world-renowned Flemish primitives. In this museum you

can see, amongst other masterpieces, *The Virgin and Child with Canon Van der Paele* by Jan van Eyck and the *Moreel Triptych* by Hans Memling. You will also marvel at the top 18th and 19th-century neoclassical pieces, masterpieces of Flemish Expressionism and post-war modern art.

**OPEN >** Tuesday to Sunday: 9.30 a.m.-5.00 p.m.; last admission: 4.30 p.m. (open on Easter Monday and Whit Monday)

**ADDITIONAL CLOSING DATES >** 1/1, 14/5 (1.00 p.m.-5.00 p.m.) and 25/12

**PRICE >** Including Arentshuis: € 8.00; 65+ and youngsters aged 12 to 25: € 6.00; children under 12: free; Brugge City Card: free

**INFORMATION >** Dijver 12, tel. +32 (0)50 44 87 43, www.museabrugge.be

## 26 Gruuthusemuseum (Gruuthuse Museum)

The luxurious city palace of the lords of Gruuthuse is closed until 2018 for extensive restoration work.

**INFORMATION >** Dijver 17, tel. +32 (0)50 44 87 43, www.museabrugge.be

## 27 Historium Bruges

What was it like to live in Bruges during the Golden Age? Experience it for yourself in the Historium. You will be transported back through time to medieval Bruges: walk around the harbour, take a look in the workshop of Van Eyck and soak up the atmosphere in the streets. Or let yourself be surprised by the delicious scents and bawdy laughter of the bathhouse. Afterwards, you can reflect on your visit while relaxing in the Duvelorium (Grand Beer Café – first floor; free Wifi) or on the panoramic terrace, where you can enjoy an unparalleled view over the Market Square.

**OPEN >** Daily, 10.00 a.m.-6.00 p.m., last admission: 5.00 p.m.

**ADDITIONAL CLOSING DATES >** 1/1, 25/12

**PRICE >** Including audio-guide (available in 9 languages): € 12.50; students (on display of a valid student card): € 9.50; children aged 2 to 14: € 7.50; Brugge City Card: free; Family Pass (2 adults and max. 3 children aged 2 to 14): € 35.00; several combination tickets possible *(See page 91)*

**INFORMATION >** Markt 1, tel. +32 (0)50 27 03 11, www.historium.be

## 09 Hof Bladelin (Bladelin Court)

In around 1440, Pieter Bladelin, treasurer of the Order of the Golden Fleece, commissioned the construction of Bladelin Court. In the 15th century the powerful Florentine banking family of De' Medici set up a branch here. The

stone medallion portraits of Lorenzo de'
Medici and his wife still grace the picturesque inner court, which was recently
restored to its former glory.

OPEN > Inner court, rooms and chapel:
Monday to Friday, 10.00 a.m.-12.00 p.m.
and 2.00 p.m.-5.00 p.m.; visits are only
possible with a guide and by appointment

ADDITIONAL CLOSING DATES >
All (Belgian) public holidays

PRICE > Inner court, rooms and chapel:
€ 5.00 (price guide not included)
Garden: € 1.00

INFORMATION > Naaldenstraat 19,
tel. +32 (0)50 33 64 34

## 🗂 08 28 Jeruzalemkapel – Adornesdomein (Jerusalem Chapel – Adornes estate)

The Adornes estate consists of the
15th-century Jerusalem Chapel (a jewel
of medieval architecture whose construction was financed by this rich merchant family), the Adornes mansion and
a series of adjacent almshouses. In the
brand-new multimedia museum, you
can follow in the footsteps of Anselm
Adornes and learn all about the world
in which he lived. You will go on a pil-

grimage, take part in a joust and meet
many notable persons of the time, such
as the King of Scotland, the Lords of
Gruuthuse and the Dukes of Burgundy.

OPEN > Monday to Saturday, 10.00 a.m.–
5.00 p.m.

ADDITIONAL CLOSING DATES >
All (Belgian) public holidays

PRICE > € 7.00; 65+: € 5.00; the disabled
people and youngsters aged 7 to 25:
€ 3.50; children under 7: free; Brugge
City Card: free

INFORMATION > Peperstraat 3A, tel. +32
(0)50 33 88 83, www.adornes.org

## 🗂 ♿ 30 Kantcentrum (Lace Centre)

Since last year, the Lace Centre has been
housed in the renovated old lace school
of the Sisters of the Immaculate Conception. The story of Bruges lace is told in
the lace museum on the ground floor.
Multimedia installations and testimonies
from international lace experts help to
explain the various different types of lace
and their geographical origin, as well as
focusing on the lace industry and lace
education in Bruges. In an interactive
way, using touch screens, the visitor is

introduced to the complexities of 'spellenwerk': the making of lace with pins and bobbins. Demonstrations (2.00 p.m.-5.00 p.m.) and various courses are organized in the lace workshop on the first floor. Please also read the interview with Kumiko Nakazaki *(See page 128)*

OPEN > Daily, 9.30 a.m.–5.00 p.m.; last admission: 4.30 p.m.; no demonstrations on Sunday

ADDITIONAL CLOSING DATES > 1/1, 14/5, 25/12; no demonstrations on the following days: 6/4, 1/5, 25/5, 21/7, 15/8, 2/11, 11/11 and 31/12

PRICE > € 5.00; youngsters aged 12 to 25 and 65+: € 4.00; children under 12: free; Brugge City Card: free

INFORMATION > Balstraat 16, tel. +32 (0)50 33 00 72, www.kantcentrum.eu

## 🏙 32 Lumina Domestica (Lamp Museum)

The museum contains the world's largest collection of lamps and lights. More than 6.000 antiques tell the complete story of interior lighting, from the torch and paraffin lamp to the light bulb and LED. The small detour into the world of luminous animals and plants is par-

ticularly interesting. In this way you can discover, for example, the light mysteries of the glow-worm, the lantern fish and the small Chinese lantern.

OPEN > Daily, 10.00 a.m.-5.00 p.m.; last admission: 4.15 p.m.

ADDITIONAL CLOSING DATES > 1/1, 5/1 to 16/1, 24/12, 25/12 and 31/12

PRICE > € 7.00; 65+ and students: € 6.00; children aged 6 to 11: € 5.00; children under 6: free; Brugge City Card: free; combination ticket possible *(See page 91)*

INFORMATION > Wijnzakstraat 2, tel. +32 (0)50 61 22 37, www.luminadomestica.be

## 🏙 ♿ 15 34 Onze-Lieve-Vrouwekerk (Church of Our Lady)

The 115.5 metres high brick tower of the Church of Our Lady is a perfect illustra-

tion of the craftsmanship of Bruges' artisans. The church displays a valuable art collection: Michelangelo's world-famous *Madonna and Child*, countless paintings, 13th-century painted sepulchres and the tombs of Mary of Burgundy and Charles the Bold. Please note that restoration work in the church is currently in progress, so it is not possible to visit the ceremonial tombs.

**OPEN >** Monday to Saturday, 9.30 a.m.-5.00 p.m.; Sunday and Holy Days, 1.30 p.m.-5.00 p.m.; last admission: 4.30 p.m., tickets for the museum section are on sale in the south transept. The church and the museum are not open to the public during nuptial and funeral masses.

**ADDITIONAL CLOSING DATES >**
Museum: 1/1, 14/5 and 25/12
**PRICE >** Church: free; museum: € 6.00;

65+ and youngsters aged 12 to 25: € 5.00; children under 12: free; Brugge City Card: free

**INFORMATION >** Mariastraat, tel. +32 (0)50 44 87 43, www.museabrugge.be

## 16 35 Onze-Lieve-Vrouw-ter-Potterie (Our Lady of the Pottery)

This hospital dates back to the 13th century, when nuns took on the care of pilgrims, travellers and the sick. In the 15th century, it evolved towards a more modern type of home for the elderly. The hospital wards with their valuable collection of works of art, monastic and religious relics and a range of objects used in nursing have been converted into a museum. The Gothic church with its baroque interior can also be visited.

**OPEN >** Tuesday to Sunday, 9.30 a.m.-12.30 p.m. and 1.30 p.m.-5.00 p.m.; last admission: 12.00 p.m. and 4.30 p.m. (open on Easter Monday and Whit Monday)

**ADDITIONAL CLOSING DATES >**
1/1, 14/5 (1.00 p.m.-5.00 p.m.) and 25/12
**PRICE >** Church: free; museum: € 4.00;

65+ and youngsters aged 12 to 25:
€ 3.00; children under 12: free; Brugge
City Card: free
INFORMATION > Potterierei 79B, tel. +32
(0)50 44 87 43, www.museabrugge.be

### 17 Onze-Lieve-Vrouw-van-Blindekenskapel (Chapel of our Lady of the Blind)

The original wooden Chapel of Our Lady
of Blindekens was erected in 1305 as an
expression of gratitude to Our Lady after
the Battle of Mons-en-Pévèle (1304). The
current chapel dates from 1651. The miraculous statue of Our Lady of Blindekens dates from the beginning of the 15th
century. In order to fulfil the 'Bruges
promise', which saw the men of the city
returned safe home after the battle, the
Blindekens procession has paraded
through the streets of the city on 15th August every year since 1305. At the end of
the parade, the people of Bruges offer a
36-pound candle in the Church of Our
Lady of the Pottery.
OPEN > Daily, 9.00 a.m.-5.00 p.m.
PRICE > Free
INFORMATION > Kreupelenstraat

### 05 37 Expo Picasso

The historic area of the former Hospital
of Saint John (Old Saint John's) hosts a
permanent exhibition of more than 120
original works of art by Pablo Picasso.
Admire the engravings and rare illustra-
tions as well as the drawings and ceramics of the world-famous artist. The exhibition outlines the evolution in his work:
from his Spanish period to cubism to sur-
realism. Also on display are some 200
works by artist friends of Picasso's, such
as Rodin, Miró, Chagall, Renoir and Mat-
isse and even a few paintings by Monet,
Toulouse-Lautrec, Degas and Braque...
OPEN > Daily, 10.00 a.m.-5.00 p.m.
ADDITIONAL CLOSING DATES >
5/1 to 30/1 and 25/12
PRICE > € 8.50; 60+ and youngsters aged
7 to 18: € 7.50; children under 7: free;
Brugge City Card: free; combination
ticket possible *(See page 91)*
INFORMATION > Old Saint John's,
Mariastraat 38, tel. +32 (0)50 47 61 08,
www.expo-brugge.be

### Seafront Zeebrugge

This maritime theme park, situated in the
unique setting of the old fish market in

Zeebrugge, allows you to explore the secrets of the sea. You will learn about the Belgian fishing industry through the interactive exhibition 'Fish, from the boat right onto your plate' and discover the bustling world of the international port of Zeebrugge. The more restful visitors can enjoy the story of coastal tourism past and present, while the adventurous can play at being the master of the West-Hinder lightship or a sailor on an authentic Russian submarine. Children can enjoy themselves on the pirate island and in the ball pool. New this year is the large commemorative exhibition 'Besieged Coast, Occupied Port – Zeebrugge & WWI' about the First World War.

OPEN > During the period 1/7 to 31/8: daily, 10.00 a.m.–6.00 p.m.; during the period 1/9 to 30/6: daily, 10.00 a.m.–5.00 p.m; adapted opening hours in winter (November/December): consult the website www.seafront.be

ADDITIONAL CLOSING DATES > 1/1, 5/1 to 23/1 and 25/12; for the annual closure period, please consult the website

PRICE > Including visit to exhibition 'Besieged Coast, Occupied Port –

Zeebrugge & WWI': € 12.50; 60+ and students (on display of a valid student card): € 11.00; children under 12: € 9.00; children up to 1 metre (accompanied by an adult): free; Brugge City Card: € 8.50

INFORMATION > Vismijnstraat 7, Zeebrugge, tel. +32 (0)50 55 14 15, www.seafront.be; public transport: train Bruges-Zeebrugge, from the station Zeebrugge-Dorp or Zeebrugge-Strand: coastal tram (direction: Knokke), stop: Kerk (Church)

## 38 Sint-Janshospitaal (Saint John's Hospital)

Saint John's Hospital has an eight hundred-year-old history of caring for pilgrims, travellers and the sick. Visit the medieval wards where the nuns and monks performed their work of mercy, as well as the chapel, and marvel at the impressive collection of archives, art works, medical instruments and six paintings by Hans Memling. Also worth a visit: the Diksmuide attic, the old dormitory, the adjoining custodian's room and the pharmacy.

OPEN > Museum: Tuesday to Sunday, 9.30 a.m.-5.00 p.m. Pharmacy: Tuesday to Sunday, 9.30 a.m.-11.45 a.m. and 2.00 p.m.-5.00 p.m., last admission both: 4.30 p.m. (both open on Easter Monday and Whit Monday)

ADDITIONAL CLOSING DATES >
1/1, 14/5 (1.00 p.m.-5.00 p.m.) and 25/12

PRICE > Including visit to the pharmacy: € 8.00; 65+ and youngsters aged 12 to 25: € 6.00; children under 12: free; Brugge City Card: free

INFORMATION > Mariastraat 38, tel. +32 (0)50 44 87 43, www.museabrugge.be

PRICE > For both mills together: € 3.00; 65+ and youngsters aged 12 to 25: € 2.00; children under 12: free; Brugge City Card: free

INFORMATION > Kruisvest, tel. +32 (0)50 44 87 43, www.museabrugge.be

## 39 Sint-Janshuismolen (Mill)
## 31 Koeleweimolen (Mill)

Windmills have graced Bruges' ramparts ever since the construction of the outer city wall at the end of the 13th century. Today four specimens are left on Kruisvest. Sint-Janshuis Mill (1770) is still in its original spot and still grinding grain just like its neighbour Koelewei Mill. These are the only two mills you can visit.

OPEN > Sint-Janshuis Mill: during the period 1/5 to 31/8: Tuesday to Sunday, 9.30 a.m.-12.30 p.m. and 1.30 p.m.-5.00 p.m., last admission: 12.00 p.m. and 4.30 p.m. (open on Whit Monday); Koelewei Mill: during the period 1/7 to 31/8: Tuesday to Sunday, 9.30 a.m.-12.30 p.m. and 1.30 p.m.-5.00 p.m., last admission: 12.00 p.m. and 4.30 p.m.

ADDITIONAL CLOSING DATE > Sint-Janshuis Mill: 14/5 (1.00 p.m.-5.00 p.m.)

## 23 Sint-Salvatorskathedraal (Saint Saviour's Cathedral)

Bruges' oldest parish church (12th– 15th century) has amongst its treasures a rood loft with an organ, medieval tombs, Brussels tapestries and a rich collection of Flemish paintings (14th- 18th century). The treasure-chamber displays, amongst others, paintings by Dieric Bouts, Hugo van der Goes and other Flemish primitives.

OPEN > Cathedral: Monday to Friday, 10.00 a.m.-1.00 p.m. and 2.00 p.m.- 5.30 p.m.; Saturday, 10.00 a.m.-1.00 p.m. and 2.00 p.m.-3.30 p.m.; Sunday, 11.30 a.m.-12.00 p.m. and 2.00 p.m.- 5.00 p.m.; the cathedral is not open to the public during masses; Treasury: daily (except Saturday), 2.00 p.m.-5.00 p.m. Useful to know: restoration work is currently being carried out in the cathedral.

MUSEUMS, PLACES OF INTEREST AND ATTRACTIONS

This can influence the opening hours of the treasure-chamber.

**ADDITIONAL CLOSING DATES** > Cathedral: 1/1 (afternoon), 14/5 (afternoon), 24/12 (afternoon) and 25/12 (afternoon). Treasury: 1/1, 14/5, 24/12 and 25/12
**PRICE** > Cathedral and Treasury: free
**INFORMATION** > Steenstraat, tel. +32 (0)50 33 61 88, www.sintsalvator.be

## **41** Schuttersgilde Sint-Sebastiaan (Saint Sebastian's Archers' Guild)

The Guild of Saint Sebastian is an archers' guild that has already been in existence for more than 600 years, which is unprecedented anywhere in the world. The members of this longbow guild are exclusively male, with two no-table exceptions: Queen Mathilde of Belgium and the Queen of England. A visit includes the royal chamber, the chapel chamber and the garden.

**OPEN** > During the period 1/5 until 30/9: Tuesday, Wednesday and Thursday, 10.00 a.m.-12.00 p.m., Saturday, 2.00 p.m.-5.00 p.m.; during the period 1/10 to 30/4: Tuesday, Wednesday, Thursday and Saturday, 2.00 p.m.-5.00 p.m.
**PRICE** > € 3.00
**INFORMATION** > Carmersstraat 174, www.sebastiaansgilde.be

## 🔲 ♿ **16** **42** Sound Factory

Visit the Sound Factory on the upper floor of the Concert Hall: let the bells of Bruges chime, or work with *samples* and sounds to create your own compositions. The roof of the Lantaarntoren not only commands a unique view across the historic city centre, but also gives you the opportunity to experiment with bells and sounds to your heart's content.

**OPEN** > Tuesday to Sunday, 9.30 a.m.-5.00 p.m.; last admission: 4.30 p.m. (open on Easter Monday and Whit Monday)

ADDITIONAL CLOSING DATES >
1/1, 14/5 (1.00 p.m.-5.00 p.m.) and 25/12
PRICE > € 6.00; 65+ and youngsters
aged 12 to 25: € 5.00; children under
12: free; Brugge City Card: free
INFORMATION > 't Zand 34,
www.sound-factory.be

## 🏛 ♿ 09 43 Stadhuis (City Hall)

Bruges' City Hall (1376) is one of the oldest in the Low Countries. It is from here that the city has been governed for more than 600 years. An absolute masterpiece is the Gothic Hall, with its late 19th-century murals and polychrome vault. The adjoining historic hall calls up the city council's history with a number of authentic documents and works of art. A multimedia exhibition on the ground floor illustrates the evolution of the Burg Square.

OPEN > Daily, 9.30 a.m.-5.00 p.m.,
last admission: 4.30 p.m.
ADDITIONAL CLOSING DATES >
1/1, 14/5 (1.00 p.m.-5.00 p.m.) and 25/12
PRICE > Including Liberty of Bruges:
€ 4.00; 65+ and youngsters aged 12
to 25: € 3.00; children under 12: free;
Brugge City Card: free
INFORMATION > Burg 12, tel. +32 (0)50 44
87 43, www.museabrugge.be

## 🏛 45 Volkskundemuseum (Folklore Museum)

These renovated 17th century, single-room dwellings accommodate, amongst other things, a classroom, a millinery, a pharmacy, a confectionery shop, a grocery shop and an authentic bedroom interior. You can also admire a beautiful lace collection on the upper floor. Every first and third Thursday of the month (except for public holidays), those with a sweet tooth can attend a demonstration given by the 'spekkenbakker' (sweet-maker). You can relax in the museum inn, 'De Zwarte Kat' (The Black Cat) or in the garden, where you can try out traditional folk games on the terrace.

OPEN > Tuesday to Sunday: 9.30 a.m.-5.00 p.m., last admission: 4.30 p.m. (open on Easter Monday and Whit Monday); the inn 'De Zwarte Kat' does not have any specific opening hours
ADDITIONAL CLOSING DATES >
1/1, 14/5 (1.00 p.m.-5.00 p.m.) and 25/12
PRICE > € 4.00; 65+ and youngsters aged 12 to 25: € 3.00; children under 12: free; Brugge City Card: free
INFORMATION > Balstraat 43, tel. +32 (0)50 44 87 43, www.museabrugge.be

# TAKE ADVANTAGE!

## » Brugge City Card

With the Bruges City Card, you get free entrance ![icon] to 27 museums and other sites of interest in the centre of Bruges and a minimum 25% discount ![icon] at various attractions and museums outside Bruges. The Brugge City Card can be purchased from the Tourist offices on ![i] 't Zand (Concertgebouw), the Markt (Market Square - Historium), and the Stationsplein (Station Square – Railway station). You can also purchase the discount card online via www.bruggecitycard.be. For more information about the Bruges City Card, see page 12.

## » Museum Pass

With the Museum Pass you can visit the different Musea Brugge locations as often as you like for just € 20.00 (www. museabrugge.be). Youngsters aged 12 to 25 pay just € 15.00. The pass is valid for three consecutive days and can be purchased at all Musea Brugge locations and at the tourist office ![i] 't Zand (Concertgebouw).

## » Combination ticket Historium/Groeninge Museum

Experience the Golden Century of Bruges in the Historium, with the painting of *Madonna and Child with Canon Joris van der Paele* by Jan van Eyck as your leitmotif. Then see the masterpiece itself in the Groeninge Museum, along with the great works of many others of the so-called Flemish primitives. This € 15.00 combination ticket is only available in the Historium.

## » Combination ticket Historium/beer tasting in the Duvelorium

Discover the Bruges of the year 1435 in the Historium and afterwards enjoy three typical Belgian beers (16 cl) in the Duvelorium Grand Beer Café. This combination ticket costs € 19.50 and is available exclusively from the Historium.

## » Combination ticket Historium/City walk

Journey through medieval Bruges in the Historium and immediately afterwards discover all the most beautiful hidden spots during a guided walk through the city. Combination ticket: € 16.50, for sale at the Historium.

## » Combination ticket Expo Picasso/Museum-Gallery Xpo Salvador Dalí

Discover the works of two top artists for just € 16.00; 60+, youngsters aged 7 to 18 and students (on display of a valid student card): € 12.50. This combination ticket is only available in the museums in question.

## » Combination ticket Choco-Story/Diamond Museum

Combine a tasty visit to Choco-Story with a dazzling look at the Diamond Museum. This combination ticket costs € 14.00. For sale at the abovementioned museums and at ![i] 't Zand (Concertgebouw).

## » Combination ticket Choco-Story/Lumina Domestica/Belgian Fries Museum

Visit these three museums at reduced rates.

- » Combination ticket Choco-Story/Frietmuseum: € 13.00; 65+ and students: € 11.00; children aged 6 to 11: € 8.00; children under 6: free
- » Combination ticket Choco-Story/Lumina Domestica: € 10.00; 65+ and students: € 9.00; children aged 6 to 11: € 7.00; children under 6: free
- » Combination ticket (3 museums): € 15.00; 65+ and students: € 13.00; children aged 6 to 11: € 10.00; children under 6: free

These combination tickets are for sale at the above-mentioned museums and at ![i] 't Zand (Concertgebouw).

# Culture and amusement

The city's high-quality cultural life flourishes as never before. Devotees of modern architecture stand in awe of the Concertgebouw (Concert hall) whilst enjoying an international top concert or an exhilarating dance performance. Romantic souls throng the elegant City Theatre for an unforgettable night. Jazz enthusiasts feel at home at Art Centre De Werf, whereas the MaZ is the place to be for young people.

## 🏙♿ 16 Concertgebouw (Concert Hall)

This international centre for music and the performing arts offers a varied programme of music and contemporary dance. The imposing Concert Hall (1,289 seats) and the intimate Chamber Music Hall (322 seats) both have outstanding acoustics. Through its interactive sound art space (Sound Factory) and the permanent exhibition of various works of art, the Concert Hall provides visitors with a variety of contemporary art experiences. Bruges City Card: a 30% discount on the productions that are indicated on the free monthly event calendar.
INFORMATION > 't Zand 34, tel. +32 (0)70 22 33 02 (ticket line: Monday to Friday, 4.30 p.m.-6.30 p.m.), www.concertgebouw.be

## 🏙♿ 44 Stadsschouwburg (City Theatre)

The Bruges City Theatre (1869) is one of the best-preserved theatres of its kind in Europe and was fully restored in 2001. The sober neo-Renaissance facade of this royal theatre conceals a palatial foyer and an equally magnificent auditorium. This outstanding infrastructure is used for performances of contemporary dance and theatre and for concerts of various kinds. Brugge City Card: a 30% discount on the productions that are indicated on the free monthly event calendar.
INFORMATION > Vlamingstraat 29, tel. +32 (0)50 44 30 60 (Monday to Friday, 1.00 p.m.-6.00 p.m. Saturday 10.00 a.m.-1.00 p.m., closed 1/7 to 15/8), www.ccbrugge.be

## 🏙♿ 33 Magdalenazaal (MaZ, Magdalena Concert Hall)

Its 'black-box' architecture means that the MaZ is the ideal location for youth events. The Bruges Cultural Centre and the Cactus Music Festival both organize pop and rock concerts here. Major artists from the world of music and more intimate club talents can all 'do their own thing' in the MaZ. Rising stars in the theatrical and dance arts also perform in this perfect setting. Children's and family events are regular features on the programme. Brugge City Card: a 30% discount on the productions that are indicated on the free monthly event calendar.
INFORMATION > Magdalenastraat 27, Sint-Andries, tel. +32 (0)50 44 30 60 (Monday to Friday, 1.00 p.m.-6.00 p.m., Saturday, 10.00 a.m.-1.00 p.m., closed 1/7 to 15/8), www.ccbrugge.be

## 🏙♿ 19 De Werf (Art Centre)

De Werf Cultural Centre has an excellent reputation in the jazz milieu and is a favourite venue for many Belgian and foreign jazz musicians. From the beginning of October to the end of May, there is a free jam session in the foyer on every second Monday of the month. De Werf is also a great place to pick up a theatre production or some other exciting podium performance. In short, this is a setting where people create, produce, present and are inspired! Brugge City Card: a 25% discount on the productions that are indicated on the free monthly event calendar.
INFORMATION > Werfstraat 108, tel. +32 (0)50 33 05 29, www.dewerf.be

# What's on the programme?

The list below shows some of the most important events taking place in Bruges. The precise dates are notified in **the free monthly event calendar**, which you can pick up at any of the city's tourist offices on the **i** Markt (Historium), 't Zand (Concertgebouw) and the Stationsplein (station). In the tourist offices, you will also find the free monthly cultural paper, Exit. And, of course, for a detailed events calendar you can always consult the website at www.visitbruges.be.

## January

### Bach Academie

The fifth Bruges Bach Academy focuses on the theme of death. How did Bach, his peers and his followers cope with ageing, dying and the question of eternal life? The repertoire of Bach and his contemporaries is performed by Collegium Vocale Ghent, Vox Luminis and numerous renowned soloists. This edition of the Bach Academy starts with two preludes, in collaboration with De Werf and the Bruges Cultural Centre.

**INFORMATION >** www.concertgebouw.be

## 14-18: THE WAR IN IMAGES | BRUGES DURING THE GREAT WAR
*City Halls (Belfry), until 22 February 2015*

With three Great War exhibitions at a single location, Bruges goes in search of its own wartime past and seeks to trace the impact – still felt today – of the terrible events that took place between 1914 and 1918. In a historical section, curator Sophie De Schaepdrijver recalls the war years in occupied Bruges through contemporary photographs and images. In a second section, Magnum photographer Carl De Keyzer gives new life to a series of 100-year-old glass negatives, from which he has made new prints, with David Van Reybrouck providing the necessary textual commentaries. In the third exhibition, ten international Magnum photographers reflect on the theme of war – a theme which, sadly enough, is still a current one. You can find more info on www.brugge.be. And visitors who really want to explore the old front region can perhaps take advantage of one of the suggestions made in the chapter 'Excursions from Bruges – In search of the Great War'. *(See page 155-158)*

## February

### Brugs Bierfestival (Bruges Beer Festival)

For a whole weekend long, you can discover Belgian beers both old and new in the Beurshalle. The festival brings together more than 65 Belgian breweries, which account for the production of more than 300 different beers.

INFORMATION >
www.brugsbierfestival.be

### Reismarkt (Travel Market)

An alternative travel fair in the City Halls. Under the motto 'Travellers help travellers', enthusiastic globetrotters exchange a wide range of tips and information about almost every type of travel and every destination you can think of.

INFORMATION > www.wegwijzer.be

## March

### Brugge Culinair (Culinary Bruges)

An exhibition for food connoisseurs and gastronomes at the Oud-Sint-Jan complex. In the different pop-up restaurants you can try out various delicious dishes and at the 'Mondo Market' you will discover a wide range of local products from all over Europe. Free entrance.

INFORMATION > www.bruggeculinair.be

## April

### Ronde van Vlaanderen (Tour of Flanders)

This historic and world-famous race for professional cyclists will take place for the 99th time in 2015. The starting point is on the Markt.

INFORMATION >
www.rondevanvlaanderen.be

### More Music!

A four-day festival of diverse musical genres in the Concert Hall, in collaboration with the Cactus Music Centre. The programme includes many big names, such as Nicolas Bernier & Martin Messier and Liesa Van der Aa.

INFORMATION >
www.moremusicfestival.be

### Mooov filmfestival

This 10-day film festival, screened in Cinema Lumière, shows the best new films from Africa, Asia and South America. The programme covers both artistically innovative movies and films with a social conscience.

INFORMATION > www.mooov.be

### Rumoer! (Noise!)

The Rumoer! event draws its inspiration from the fascination and fear people have for noise in times of war. Some of the works are performed with a link to the Great War; others are futuristic compositions. Traditional forms of concert presentation, sound installations and theatre performances.

INFORMATION > www.concertgebouw.be

## May

### Meifoor (May Fair)

For three fun-filled weeks some 90 fairground attractions 'take over' 't Zand, the Beursplein, the Koning Albertpark and the Simon Stevinplein.

### Ascension Day – Heilig Bloedprocessie (Procession of the Holy Blood)

Since 1304, this popular procession through the city has portrayed scenes from the Old and New Testament. Of course, the procession has undergone changes over the centuries, but its essential religious purpose – the commemoration of the suffering of Christ – has been preserved. The Procession of the Holy Blood has been included in the UNESCO list for the intangible cultural heritage of humanity since 2009.

### Dwars door Brugge (Running through Bruges)

Thousands of runners set off on a 15 km route through the city. This unique running event through the historic centre of Bruges is no longer just popular with local people, but now attracts competitors from all over the world. For the lesser gods, there is a 5 km course and a Kids Run is organized for children up to 12 years of age.

INFORMATION > www.brugge.be

### Budapest Festival

A three-day festival of music with concerts by the renowned Budapest Festival Orchestra, conducted by Iván Fischer. Each musical piece performed by Fischer and his orchestra gains a new dimension. Not surprisingly, the Budapest Festival Orchestra is regarded as one of the ten best orchestras in the world. A must for all music-lovers.

INFORMATION > www.concertgebouw.be

## June

### Triathlon Bruges

This quarter triathlon (1 km swimming, 45 km cycling and 10 km running) through the city centre and the area around Bruges is being organised for the 12th time this year. The event is exceptional because the swimming part takes place in the city's picturesque canals ('reien') and the athletes pass numerous famous tourist spots, such as the Rozenhoedkaai, the Dijver, the Burg, the Market Square, etc.

INFORMATION > www.triatlonbrugge.be

## TRIENNIAL OF CONTEMPORARY ART AND ARCHITECTURE BRUGES 2015

A series of 'radical' works of art by internationally renowned artists and architects, spread across the city centre, will encourage visitors to reflect on current global urbanisation and on the role that can be played by an old, small-scale city like Bruges in helping to make the megalopolises of the future more liveable. Until mid-October.

INFORMATION > www.triennalebrugge.be *(More on page 100)*

## CARILLON CONCERTS

Throughout the year, you can enjoy free, live carillon concerts in Bruges on Wednesdays, Saturdays and Sundays from 11.00 a.m. to 12.00 p.m. From mid-June to mid-September, evening concerts also take place on Mondays and Wednesdays from 9.00 p.m. to 10.00 p.m. The inner courtyard of the Belfry is a good place to listen. *(Also read the interview on p. 104 with city carillonneur Frank Deleu)*
INFORMATION >
www.carillon-brugge.be

### Feest in 't Park (Party in the Park)

A free, family-friendly festival in the Minnewaterpark, with a children's world village, workshops, world cooking and plenty of music, theatre and dance.
INFORMATION > www.feestintpark.be

## July

### Vama Veche

This free multi-day music festival in the Koningin Astridpark kicks off the summer. The festival is named after a small Romanian village by the Black Sea, Vama Veche, which means 'old customs'. After the fall of the Iron Curtain, it was the first place where young musicians could perform freely.
INFORMATION > www.vamaveche.be

### Zandfeesten (Zand Festival)

Flanders' largest antiques and second-hand market on 't Zand, the Beursplein and in the Koning Albertpark attracts bargain-hunters from far and wide.

### Cactus Festival

This attractive open air festival in the Minnewater Park serves up a cocktail of rock, reggae, world music and dance. Notwithstanding its international fame, the three-day festival manages to preserve a cosy and familial atmosphere, with numerous fun activities for children.
INFORMATION > www.cactusfestival.be

### Navy Days

In Zeebrugge, under the watchful eye of sailors from home and abroad, you can hop from one impressive ship to another during this two-day regatta with numerous free exhibitions and demonstrations.
INFORMATION > www.mil.be/navycomp

### Moods!

For two full weeks, you can enjoy musical and other fireworks at unforgettable locations in Bruges city centre. The programme includes concerts, 'Leg Work' ('Benenwerk' - dance) and 'Perfect Performing Pubs' ('Klinkende Kroegen' - performances in or near more than 20 of the city's most enjoyable pubs). Many of the activities are free of charge.

INFORMATION > www.moodsbrugge.be; www.benenwerk.be; www.brugge.be/klinkende_kroegen

## August

### Zandfeesten (Zand Festival)

Antiques and second-hand market on 't Zand, the Beursplein and in the Koning Albertpark *(See above)*.

### Bruges Lace Days

From mid-August, the Walplein and the buildings of the Halve Maan Brewery buzz with lace activities: information and exposition stands, lace sale and demonstrations. Free entry.

INFORMATION > www.kantcentrum.eu *(You read more about lace on page 83-84 – Lace Centre and in the interview with Kumiko Nakazaki, page 128)*

### MAfestival

Each year this highly respected festival of ancient music – MA stands for Musica Antiqua – continues to attract the world's top performers to Bruges and Bruges' Hinterland.

INFORMATION > www.mafestival.be

### Lichtfeest (Festival of Light)

During the Light Festival, Lissewege becomes more fairytale-like than ever: as soon as night falls, thousands of little candles are lit in the centre of the white village. Poetry, background music, intimate fire installations, street art and street theatre complete the romantic picture.

INFORMATION > www.bruggeplus.be

### Uitzomeren (Goodbye summer!)

During the last weekend of August, people can wave goodbye to the summer holidays at the child-friendly 'Uitzomeren' festival, which provides a mix of street theatre, film (evening) and music. The programme features a large picnic on Sunday. The place to be: Sebrechtspark, entrance via Oude Zak. Free of charge.

INFORMATION > www.bruggeplus.be

## September

### Open Monumentendag (Open Monument Day)

During the second weekend of September, Flanders organises the 27th edition of Open Monument Day, when it opens the doors of its many monuments to the general public.

INFORMATION > www.openmonumenten.be

### 'Kroenkelen' on Car-free Sunday

During the Kroenkelen happening, cyclists and walkers can re-discover the pleasure of a car-free inner city (10.00 a.m.–6.00 p.m.) and the green fringe around Bruges. There are rest places along the route, where the participants can take a breather and 'strengthen the inner man' (or woman), while enjoying some fine music and entertainment.

INFORMATION > www.brugge.be

### Zandfeesten (Zand Festival)

Antiques and second-hand market on 't Zand, the Beursplein and in the Koning Albertpark *(See above)*.

## October

### Kookeet (Cook-eat)

The fifth edition of Kookeet, with star-chef Geert Van Hecke as its 'godfather', will take place in early October in a stylish tented village on 't Zand. During this three-day culinary event, thirty of Bruges' gourmet chefs will serve various gastronomic dishes at fair prices.

INFORMATION > www.kookeet.be

### Brugge Urban Trail

The Bruges Urban Trail is a unique 10 km running event, taking in several of the city's beautiful parks and many of its important historic buildings. By running and jumping your way around the course, you will discover these tourist gems and magnificent monuments in a highly original manner!

INFORMATION > www.sport.be/bruggeurbantrail

## November

### Razor Reel Flanders Film Festival

A two-week festival of fun for fantasy movie-lovers: from fairy-tale fantasies to frightening horror movies, from new releases to classics of the genre and true cult movies. Besides film screenings, there are also workshops, exhibitions and a fantasy movie and book fair.

INFORMATION > www.rrfff.be

## December

### Christmas Market and ice-rink

For a whole month you can soak up the Christmas atmosphere on the Markt (Market Square) at the Simon Stevin-plein; on the Market Square you can even pull on your ice-skates and glide gracefully around the temporary rink in the shadow of the Belfry.

### December Dance

A contemporary dance festival that allows renowned choreographers to 'do their own thing'. For ten days, dance-lovers will be treated to a sensual confrontation between the contemporary and the traditional, between slow and fast, between sound and silence, between spirituality and exuberance.

INFORMATION > www.decemberdance.be

### Bruges Christmas Run

This unique running event (6 or 10 km) for charity celebrates its 5th edition in 2015. The course takes runners through the festively illuminated city centre and starts at 8.00 p.m. on the Market Square.

INFORMATION > www.lopenvoorhetgoededoel.be

## Take advantage!

With the Bruges City Card you can benefit from a discount on many events. You can find full details in the free events calendar issued by the City Bruges.

*(For more information, see page 12)*

Triennial of Contemporary Art and Architecture, Bruges 2015

Cracking the City Gene - from 20 May to 18 October 2015

# Bruges as an example for the world

For the first time, a Contemporary Art and Architecture Triennial is being organised in Bruges. This is not just the first edition of a three-yearly event, but an impressive, ground-breaking art project.

As of 2007, more than half of the world's population now live in cities. From the trendy skyscrapers of Tokyo to the impersonal tower blocks of Beijing and the overcrowded favelas of Rio de Janeiro. These rapidly expanding urban centres, often with many millions of inhabitants, are constantly in motion and constantly evolving. In this context, the timeless and unchanging character of Bruges can be regarded as the opposite of this endless, non-stop dynamic. The Triennial brings to life these very different types of city in the historic centre of Bruges, which results in a fascinating series of artistic encounters and confrontations.

## Unique confrontations

Over 40 artists, architects, scientists and policy makers from home and abroad are currently working on this theme. Starting from May 2015, they will exhibit a series of thought-provoking works on the streets and squares of Bruges. The works will include new creations by, amongst others, Bruce Odland (United States), Sam Auinger (Austria), together O+A, Atelier Bow-Wow (Japan), Tadashi Kawamata (Japan), Studio Mumbai (India), Anne Senstad (Norway), Vibeke Jensen (Norway), Nathan Coley (United Kingdom),

TRIËNNALE
BRUGGE 2015

WWW.TRIENNALEBRUGGE.BE

Nicolas Grenier (Canada) and many others. Their works – or rather 'interventions' – are concentrated in three 'archipelagos', spread along a north-south axis running through the city. These interventions are not only architectural and sculptural; the public spaces in Bruges will also play host to sound systems and 'urban interventions' as well. Alongside the swans in the city moats, which are such an integral part of the intimate charm of Bruges, some new, intriguing and occasionally alienating works of art will also be displayed, confusing you for just a few seconds, before leading to a moment of reflection and thought.

## Challenge

The Triennial challenges us to think outside the box. 'What if ...?' What if the more than five million people that visit Bruges each year should suddenly decide to live here permanently? What if they would just stay? Bruges would immediately be transformed into a fast growing, multicultural metropolis, with all the possibilities and challenges that this entails. It would inevitably lead to problems in many fields, such as housing, ecology, mobility and energy. But at the same time, it would also create a powerful dynamic, a city full of cultural diversity and human potential. This duality is already a reality in many of the world's megalopolises.

## Bruges, where all the cities of the world come together

The themes of the Triennial are further explored in various indoor exhibitions. This allows the visitor not only to obtain information about the ongoing Triennial and its international participants, but also to view well-known plans and models for 'ideal' cities and inspect key documents outlining utopian urban polices from past and for the future. In this way, the works and personal stories of the different artists, architects, scientists, policy makers and members of the public are connected to one another. This will result in a series of new, utopian – or, if necessary, dystopian – stories about Bruges as a temporary, imaginary megalopolis; the city where all the cities of the world come together.

Eiermarkt

# Tips from
# **Bruges**
# **connoisseurs**

# Working with the best view over Bruges, World Heritage City
## Baroque in the air

Frank Deleu, mad about music, knew how to make use of his passion. He is Bruges' carilloneur and he was a producer at Klara, the classical radio broadcasting station. As he is also an enthusiastic bon vivant who likes to wander through the city and her glorious past, it is abundantly clear that he is a unique personality who knows everything about Bruges' immaterial heritage and the history of her most famous tower.

## IDENTIKIT

**Name:** Frank Deleu
**Nationality:** Belgian
**Date of birth:** 23 August 1952
Has lived in Bruges since 1984.
The city's carilloneur, the man with the loftiest place of work in the historic city centre.

Frank Deleu looks down on Bruges; literally, that is. At least three times a week, the city's carilloneur climbs the three hundred and sixty-six steps of the belfry to reach his place of work. A long, 'uphill' walk that takes him eight minutes (providing visitors don't hold him up) and eventually brings him to his unique percussion instrument. The 47 bells date mainly from the 18th century and have recently been restored. But in spite of his lonely place of work, the city bell-ringer is anything but a loner. 'It's just part and parcel of my job to play an instrument high and dry above the crowds. I don't do it for the applause, of course, I wouldn't hear it anyway. It's more of a passion that has grown on me.'

This iconic building – in medieval Flanders the belfries were regarded as a symbol of civic liberty – may have lost its original function of telling local people the time, but the carillon remains immensely popular with natives and visitors alike. In summer the evening recitals attract large crowds to the belfry's courtyard. Others prefer to listen to the sound of the bells at their own favourite spots in the city. The narrow Breidelstraat is one such spot, with its near-perfect acoustics, while listeners on the Burg also sit on the front row, musically speaking! Many writers have also sung the praises of the carillon of Bruges. Some of them were world-famous, such as Henry Wadsworth Longfellow, Charles Baudelaire and Jules Verne. Le carilloneur de Bruges even inspired three operas. And during the mid-19th century many English visitors came especially to Bruges, then the poorest city in the country, just to listen to the bells.

## 'Tower of Sounds'

Each day Frank Deleu is filled with admiration for the beauty that Bruges has managed to preserve, the concen-

*'Not only has Bruges been perfectly preserved in time, the streets are also kept very tidy.'*

tration of her museums and art works, her many intimate historical places and her busy cultural agenda. 'Not only has Bruges been perfectly preserved in time, the streets are also kept very tidy. I therefore hope that the city will be able to look after her his-torical face in the future, Like many of the Italian cities have done: by re-stricting traffic and keep away contemporary architectural experiments. There is plenty of room for them away from the city centre.'

But this does not mean that the city bell

## VIA BRUGENSIS

History is literally to be found on the cobbles of Brug-es' streets, that is to say along the forty scallops that form the Bruges section of the Via Brugensis – the an-cient pilgrims' route to Santiago de Compostela. The scallops are a modest homage to the thousands of pilgrims that have followed the route from the region of the Zwin via Bruges, Menin and Tournai to Sebourg near Valenciennes in the north of France, where they used to join the GR long-distance footpath.

## SUMMERY CARILLON SOUNDS

The visitor who wishes to listen to Frank Deleu from the most advantageous spot should hasten to the courtyard of the Belfry on a Monday or Wednesday evening during the summer months. The recital kicks off at 9.00 p.m. For the next hour the carilloneur will then indulge in his passion for his unique instrument. Deleu also plays the carillon throughout the year from 11.00 to 12.00 a.m. on Wednesday, Saturday and Sunday.

*(You can find more information about the carillon concerts on page 97)*

ringer is against innovation and modernity. For example, he is very enthusiastic about the Sound Factory, an interactive space for aural art on the panoramic roof of the Concertgebouw (Concert Hall). To celebrate 500 years of the carilloneur's art, an inventory was made of all the bells in the historic city centre. The name of the maker and the place of manufacture were established for each bell, following which its own unique sound was recorded. Via two interactive touch screens, visitors can use these sounds to compose their own carillion concert and then listen to it being played over the city.

*(See page 89 for all practical information on the Sound Factory)*

# Frank Deleu
## Best addresses

## FAVOURITE SPOT

» **Onze-Lieve-Vrouw-ter-Potterie**, Potterierei 79B, www.museabrugge. be, closed on Monday

'The most moving place in town is the museum and **church of Our Lady of the Pottery**, a slightly out-of-the way spot, but one that well rewards the effort of finding it. The building is filled to the brim with jewels from a bygone age, from 16<sup>th</sup>-century household goods to furniture and unique paintings that time seems to have forgotten.'

## RESTAURANTS

» **Diligence**, Hoogstraat 5, tel. +32 (0)50 33 16 60, closed on Tuesday and Wednesday

'I am a big fan of the simple and authentic spontaneity of the Diligence. No matter who walks in through the door, the welcome is always warm and friendly, and they are immediately shown to a cosy table in this somewhat dark but always hospitable restaurant. No unnecessary fuss and frills. Just plain and simple Flemish dishes that will leave you wanting more.'

» **Restaurant Pergola**, Meestraat 7, tel. +32 (0)50 44 76 50, www.restaurantpergola.be, closed on Tuesday and Wednesday

'Bruges has many delightful terraces, but the terrace at Restaurant Pergola certainly comes in the top ten. Here, far from the noise of the crowds, you can admire the solemn beauty of the Groenerei, while sampling one of the restaurant's excellent and inventive dishes. Satisfaction guaranteed!'

» **Sint-Joris**, Markt 29, tel. +32 (0)50 33 30 62, www.restaurant-sintjoris.be,
   closed on Tuesday evening (from 5.00 p.m. onwards) and Wednesday

'Some people love top-quality gastronomic fireworks, but I prefer simple and
tasty cooking. Such as the delicious everyday dishes you can find in the Sint-
Joris. Its convenient and picturesque location on the Market Square makes it
worth the recommendation alone!'

» **Carlito's**, Hoogstraat 21, tel. +32 (0)50 49 00 75, www.carlitos.be,
   no closing day

'Nothing is simpler yet more delicious than a really good pizza. Not too much
topping, but just the right amount of day-fresh ingredients. Carlo also makes
plenty of great-tasting pasta dishes, but I always go for one of those perfect piz-
zas. The simple things in life are often the best. Basta!'

» **Trattoria Trium**, Academiestraat 23, tel. +32 (0)50 33 30 60,
   www.trattoriatrium.be, closed on Monday

'Every visit to Trium is a real experience. As soon as you enter, you think you are
in Naples. Complete with gesticulating Italian waiters, who demonstrate all the
flare and passion for which their native country is famous! Trium guarantees atmosphere and theatricality by the bucketful, which perfectly complements their
honest and authentic pasta.'

## CAFÉS

» **Craenenburg**, Markt 16,
   tel. +32 (0)50 33 34 02,
   www.craenenburg.be,
   no closing day

'Craenenburg is the last "real" café on
the Market Square. It was from this
building that Margaret of York followed
the great tournament of 1468. And it was also from here that Maximilian of Austria was forced to watch the torture and execution of his own sheriff and counsellor. Today, it is a favourite spot for local people, where they can catch up on all
the latest city gossip and news.'

» **Concertgebouwcafé**, 't Zand 34, tel. +32 (0)50 47 69 81,
www.concertgebouw.be/en/cafe, closed on Sunday, Monday and Tuesday
'The Concertgebouwcafé (at the Concert Hall) is the ideal place to enjoy an after-performance drink and chat. This trendy bar has real star-quality! Enjoy a coffee or some of their great finger food as you watch the rest of the world pass by outside.'

» **Cultuurcafé Biekorf**, Naaldenstraat 4, tel. +32 (0)499 32 64 78,
www.brugge.be, closed on Sunday
'You can find this café on the inner courtyard between the city's cultural centre and the main library. It can be reached via both these buildings, and also from the Naaldenstraat. Why not give it a try? If you're lucky, you might drop in on one of their regular surprise acts.'

» **'t Hof van Rembrandt**, Eiermarkt 10, tel. +32 (0)50 33 74 50,
www.thofvanrembrandt.be, no closing day
''t Hof van Rembrandt is the 'place to be' for real beer-lovers. The café offers a wide selection of the finest beers in Belgium. In summer, you can enjoy the pleasant outdoor terrace. In winter, you can sip your pint next to the comfort of a blazing open hearth.'

» **'t Klein Venetië**, Braambergstraat 1, tel. +32 (0)475 72 52 25, no closing day
''t Klein Venetië well deserves its name. The café has magnificent views of the city's canals and the Rozenhoedkaai. This is one of the most photographed locations in Bruges – so remember to smile!'

## SHOPPING LIST

» **Rombaux**, Mallebergplaats 13,
tel. +32 (0)50 33 25 75,
www.rombaux.be, closed on
Sunday and Monday morning
and public holidays
'This jam-packed music temple has
been promoting classical music, jazz
and top-quality contemporary music in Bruges for three generations. In all that time, the interior has hardly changed, apart from an occasional lick of paint. There is no better place to seek expert advice about really good music.'

» **Raaklijn**, Kuipersstraat 1, tel. +32 (0)50 33 67 20,
www.boekhandelraaklijn.be, closed on Sunday

'The Raaklijn Book Store is a home from home for literature fans. It's a place where you can nose around for hours, just enjoying the pleasure of looking for what you want. And usually you will find something to tickle your fancy!'

» **Callebert**, Wollestraat 25, tel. +32 (0)50 33 50 61, www.callebert.be,
closed on Sunday morning and Monday morning

'A design-lover like me can always find something of interest at Callebert's. Iittala glass work, Alessi gadgets, Georg Jensen cutlery, a Stelton wine cooler, a bright pink pouffe from Quinze&Milan or a streamlined chair from Verner Panton: Callebert's has it all – and much more besides! Sometimes I hardly know where to start.'

» **I Love Coffee**, Sint-Jakobsstraat 10, tel. +32 (0)498 51 63 40,
www.ilovecofee.be, closed on Monday morning (until 12.00 p.m.)

'This brand new espresso bar not only has a beautiful interior, but also serves delicious coffee. Hardly surprising, since all the coffee beans are roasted on site. If you want to enjoy "the cup that cheers" in the privacy of your own home, you can buy one of the many fragrant, freshly-ground coffee mixes. But my favourite option is to take the time to savour a piping-hot espresso in the bar itself.'

» **Antique Shop Lieven Moenaert 'Het Brugse Vrije'**, Burg 15 -
Galerij Ter Steeghere, tel. +32 (0)497 75 33 98, lievenmoenaert@hotmail.com,
closed on Sunday and Monday and every morning (until 2.00 p.m.)

'This antique shop is a veritable treasure house of old books, documents and sculptures. The collection of artifacts is so impressive you might almost think you were in a museum! A must for all antique lovers.'

---

## SECRET TIP

» **Concertgebouw**, 't Zand 34 , tel. +32 (0)50 47 69 99, www.concertgebouw.be
'Every year the Concertgebouw (Concert Hall) manages to charm friend and foe alike with its varied programme of the very highest quality. I am particularly looking forward to the annual Bach Academy at the end of January as well as the dozens of other concerts that take place throughout the year. What's more, a visit to the Sound Factory is always great fun, because it allows you to be creative with different noises and sounds. You can experiment as much as you like.'

# Photogenic Bruges

## Andy McSweeney shows us
## the most beautiful spots in the city

His first visit to Bruges, now more than 15 years ago, made such an impression on Andy McSweeney, a Canadian with Irish roots, that he immediately fell in love with the beauty of the place - and decided to stay and marry a local girl. Nowadays, he guides photography enthusiasts who are still willing to learn around the city and shows them all the most photogenic spots.

IDENTIKIT

**Name:** Andy McSweeney
**Nationality:** Canadian
**Date of birth:** 8th December
Has lived in Bruges since 2000. Andy runs
Photo Tour Bruges. In this way, he combines
his love for Bruges with his love for photography.

It quickly became clear that Andy McSweeney, born in Montreal, was not destined to spend his whole life in Canada. At an early age, he drifted off to India, Australia and Europe, where, now more than a decade ago, he met his future wife in an Irish pub in Bruges. In almost every part of the world he has worked in catering, performed as a DJ ('I was the only one with good records') and... photographed the special places he encountered. During these wanderings he gradually trained himself to become a photographer, specializing in travel photography. 'Life as it is', perceived through a pair of keen eyes.

Andy quickly gave up on his catering and DJ career in order to focus fully on photography. And there is no better place to photograph time after time than Bruges. Nowadays, the Canadian organises *photo tours* through the city, in which he assists his clients with technical and artistic advice, while showing them all the most beautiful spots of Bruges. 'My strolls through the city are real workshops. Some of the participants are amateurs, trying to learn the basic tricks of the trade, whereas others are experienced photographers, who want to discover the most photogenic places the city has to offer. And there are plenty of those to keep them happy!' What's more, Andy McSweeney is convinced that Bruges is one of the best cities in the world to explore by camera. 'Bruges is a safe city. You don't have to be afraid that someone is going to steal your expensive camera. And the city has such beauty to offer, both past and present, at

every moment of the day and in every season. While you are taking pictures, you look at the city with very different eyes and learn to focus on details that you might otherwise miss.'

The fact that Andy first saw the light of day on the other side of the ocean he regards as an advantage. 'Anyone who is born and raised here is used to all the splendour from an early age, so that they find it harder to take a fresh look at the city. I have seen many other parts of the world, as a result of which I can probably see more easily than they can what makes this city so special. I am convinced that I can see things that they can't.'

## BRUGES ON THE BIG SCREEN

The fairytale-like and mysterious setting of Bruges has charmed numerous directors throughout the years. *The Nun's Story*, a movie from 1959 starring Audrey Hepburn, the prestigious British costume drama *The White Queen* (2013), the German romantic movie *Ein Herz aus Schokolade* (2010) and the Bollywood film *Peekay* (2014) were all shot in Bruges, as was the criminal comedy *In Bruges* (2008), which won an award for its original script. Time and again the world heritage city has been chosen as the setting for film productions or tourist shoots. The most popular filming locations are the courtyard of the Belfry, the Market Square with its Provincial Court, the Wijngaardplein, the Jerusalem Chapel and the Gothic Chamber of the Town Hall. In addition to the 'classics' (Rozenhoedkaai, Beguinage, Burg, Market Square, Minnewater and the canals), the tourist reports like to portray the lace-makers and chocolatiers of Bruges, as well as the windmills, the Church of Our Lady and the Holy Blood Basilica. Panoramic shots are taken from the roof of the Concert Hall or the Halve Maan Brewery.

## ANDY'S 5 MOST ROMANTIC PHOTOGRAPHIC HOTSPOTS

1. **Groenerei** (City map: F8) – A typical view of old bridges and historic buildings, framed by just a hint of nature.

2. **Koningin Astridpark** (City map: G9) – This classic park is a hidden gem, with its small pond with fountain and the colourful kiosk.

3. **Jan van Eyckplein** (City map: F6) –This was once the commercial heart of the city. Nowadays, it is a very pleasant spot to pass a few hours.

4. **Gruuthuse** (City map: E9) – The beautiful courtyard of the 15th century palace enfolds you in the wealth and luxury of a bygone age.

5. **Bonifaciusbrug** (City map: E9) – The charming and picturesque Bonifacius Bridge, with the Arentshof alongside, never fails to charm visitors with its sense of history and romance.

# The photographer – not the camera – determines the result

When Andy is not busy taking groups around, you will regularly see him wandering through the city on his own, either on foot or on his recumbent bicycle. 'A part of my job is to search for new and interesting views. Bruges has a lot of imposing monuments and landmarks, but the trick is to find the best way to photograph them. I always try to maintain a fresh view and pass this on to my "students". You have to leave the beaten paths, because it is here, away from the hustle and bustle, that you will find the real magic. On the Jan van Eyckplein, for example, you can be inspired by the Flemish primitives. In the tranquil Sint-Anna district we focus on classic lines. The important thing is that you don't plan too far ahead, but just let the moment happen.' And he has some other tips for future photographers: 'You don't need to own an expensive camera to take beautiful pictures. It is not the car that matters, it's the driver. And be critical: don't show your friends twenty different pictures, but just a single fantastic shot. Then they'll probably want to come to Bruges next year as well!'
*[Read more about the Photo Tour Brugge on page 67]*

*'Bruges has such beauty to offer, both past and present, at every moment of the day and in every season.'*

# Andy McSweeney
## Best addresses

## FAVOURITE SPOT

» **The Ramparts**

'I love **the Ramparts** surrounding the city and especially the stately windmills that remind us of past times. The turning sails exude a kind of peace and once you reach the top of the hill you are rewarded with a fantastic view over the city, all for free!'

---

## RESTAURANTS

» **Bierbrasserie Cambrinus**, Philipstockstraat 19, +32 (0)50 33 23 28, www.cambrinus.eu, no closing day

'This beer brasserie honours its traditional Belgian roots. Here you can choose from an extensive range of 400 different Belgian beers, served with local dishes based on Belgian beers.'

» **Bistro Pro Deo**, Langestraat 161, tel. +32 (0)50 33 73 55, www.bistroprodeo.be, closed on Sunday and Monday

'A small workers house dating from 1562 now accommodates a cosy restaurant, frequented by both tourists and local people. In this bistro, you can enjoy traditional Belgian cuisine and fresh daily produce, made the way your grandmother used to make it.'

» **Parkrestaurant**, Minderbroedersstraat 1, tel. +32 (0)497 80 18 72, www.parkrestaurant.be, closed on Monday, Thursday and during the day (until 7.00 p.m.)

'The magnificent building housing the Park Restaurant is right on the edge of the Koningin Astridpark, one of the most romantic spots of Bruges. This restaurant offers Belgian cuisine with French influences.'

» **Restaurant 't Gulden Vlies**, Mallebergplaats 17, +32 (0)50 33 47 09, www.tguldenvlies.be, closed on Sunday, Monday, Tuesday and during the day (until 7.00 p.m.)

'There are still some certainties in life. One of them is that the Gulden Vlies will open its doors at 7 o' clock in the evening, from Wednesday to Saturday, and that you will be served food of the very highest quality. It's great for either a quick snack or a more intimate dinner. A really good evening-only restaurant.'

» **Pomperlut**, Minderbroedersstraat 26, +32 (0)50 70 86 26, www.pomperlut.be, closed on Sunday and Monday

'If you want to step into another world, reserve a table at the magical Pomperlut. Small, but beautiful. Prepare yourself for gastronomic and visual indulgence on a grand scale!'

## CAFÉS

» **(Eet)café 't Hof van Beroep**, Langestraat 125, tel. +32 (0)485 68 90 33, www.thofvanberoep.com, no closing day, but closed during the day (until 4.00 p.m.)

'The Langestraat has many pubs, but the Hof van Beroep is the one that stands out. A class establishment where there is always plenty of atmosphere, with an interesting mix of locals and tourists. They have an excellent gin & tonic list and also serve great tapas and a delicious lasagne.'

» **Staminee De Garre**, De Garre 1, tel. +32 (0)50 34 10 29, www.degarre.be, no closing day, but closed every morning (until 12.00 p.m. or 11.00 a.m. on Saturday)
'This historic pub is hidden in the smallest street in Bruges and has a fine selection of delicious regional beers, as well as six draft beers, abbey beers, bottled beers and Trappist beers. Don't forget to try the tasty tapas.'

» **Joey's Café**, Zilversteeg 4, tel. +32 (0)50 34 12 64, closed on Sunday and every morning (until 11.30 a.m.)
'Local shoppers who have a sudden urge to hear a touch of the blues, jazz or rock, all hurry to this small 'brown' bar. It is located in the centre of the modern Zilverpand precinct, but is no less authentic for that. Concerts are regularly organised here.'

» **'t Brugs Beertje**, Kemelstraat 5, tel. +32 (0)50 33 96 16, www.brugsbeertje.be, closed on Tuesday, Wednesday and every morning (until 4.00 p.m.)
'The Brugs Beertje is a genuine classic, professionally managed by Daisy. This is the perfect address for anyone who wants to immerse themselves in Belgian beer culture. The beers can be accompanied by local farmhouse pâté or a Belgian cheese platter.'

» **L'Estaminet**, Park 5, tel. +32 (0)50 33 09 16, www.estaminetbrugge.be, no closing day, but closed every morning (until 11.30 a.m. and until 4.00 p.m. on Thursday afternoon)
'A classic watering-hole for Bruges pub-hoppers. The interior is dressed up as an old-fashioned living room, where you can find excellent draft beer, good music and delicious bar food. In short, L'Estaminet has everything a good pub needs.'

## SHOPPING LIST

» **LeeLoo**, Sint-Jakobsstraat 19, tel. +32 (0)50 34 04 55, www.leeloo.be, closed on Sunday
'LeeLoo is not only a trendy city boutique, but a *cool* shop with a soul inspired by the alternative fashion scene of London, Barcelona and Berlin. Clearly one step ahead of the rest.'

» **Think Twice**, Sint-Jakobsstraat 21, tel. +32 (0)495 36 39 08,
  www.thinktwice-secondhand.be, closed on Sunday morning (until 1.00 p.m.)
'Vintage lovers and bargain hunters can browse for hours in this trendy second-
hand shop that proves that nice outfits don't necessarily have to be expensive.
Definitely a place to pop into on a regular basis.'

» **Tuyttens**, Noordzandstraat 52-56, tel. +32 (0)50 44 40 10, www.tuyttens.be,
  closed on Sunday
'Every photographer has to decide for himself which camera suits him the
best. This is no easy task, considering the enormous number of different models on the market. At Tuyttens, you are provided with honest and understanda-
ble technical advice. I often come here to buy lenses, batteries, memory cards,
etc. In addition, Tuyttens also offers an excellent photo service.'

» **Depot d'O**, Riddersstraat 21, tel. +32 (0)495 23 65 95, www.depotdo.be, closed
  on Tuesday, Wednesday and Sunday and every morning (until 2.00 p.m.)
'In Depot d'O you can find great design classics, as well as African masks,
zebra carpets, animal skulls and more unusual ornaments. It is a house of
rarities, with a collection of objects that covers the entire world and an ever-
changing display window. You have to be very quick, though.'

» **Kringwinkel** 't Rad, Langestraat 169/171, tel. +32 (0)50 34 94 00,
  www.dekringwinkeltrad.be, closed on Sunday and Monday
'This second-hand store is a fantastic place for anyone who likes rummaging
around and hunting for bargains. Sometimes you can find real treasures here,
sometimes your search will lead to nothing – but it will always be pure enjoyment.'

## SECRET TIP

» **Bruges during the winter**
'For me, Bruges is at its most beautiful
when it is covered in snow. In the winter, the city moves at a more relaxed
place, landscapes are transformed into
frozen fairy tales and everywhere in the
city you see smiling faces. In this way,
Bruges becomes even more of a paradise for photographers!'

# Flemish primitives in the spotlight

Till-Holger Borchert sees respect as the key to succes

He was born in Hamburg, he lives in Brussels and he thoroughly enjoys his work in Bruges as he finds himself surrounded by six centuries of fine arts, and especially the magnificent masterpieces of the Flemish primitives. In 2002, Till-Holger Borchert was one of the curators of Bruges, Cultural Capital of Europe. Today he is chief curator of the Groeninge Museum and the Arentshuis.

## IDENTIKIT

**Name:** Till-Holger Borchert
**Nationality:** German
**Date of birth:** 4 January 1967
This chief curator of the Groeninge Museum lives in Brussels but works in Bruges. He is the author of countless publications on the Flemish primitives.

'Bruges is an exceptionally beautiful city,' says Till-Holger Borchert. 'What's more, it is also a wonderfully liveable place, partly because of the clever and careful way in which the city has been able to mix her medieval character with a modern ambiance. As early as the 13th century, the concentration of wealthy citizens enabled Bruges to become the commercial heart of North-western Europe. In the 15th century, the Burgundian authorities took successful structural measures, which resulted in an increase of the population and had a positive effect on the city's further development. Just as importantly, Bruges was spared of the any ravages of the so-called Iconoclastic Fury, which caused so much damage in other cities. That spirit of respect and tolerance still pervades the city today. I must say it is a great joy to be here. The countless locals and visitors will surely fully agree with me.'

*'Nearly every day I go
and greet two masterpieces.'*

## Madonnas from
## around the Corner

'Nearly every day I go and greet two
masterpieces: Jan van Eyck's *Madonna
with Canon Joris van der Paele* at the
Groeninge Museum and Hans Memling's *Madonna and Maarten van Nieuwenhove* at the Saint John's Hospital.
I am not saying that I discover something new every time I look at them, but
my curiosity and my pleasure remain as
great as ever. And I still try and find out
new things about them. They just continue to fascinate me! I sometimes won-

### INTERESTING TOMBS

The central feature in the Jerusalem
Chapel – located in the charming
Sint-Anna district – is the ceremonial
tomb of Anselm Adornes (1424-1483)
and his wife, Margaretha Vander Banck
(d. 1462). Anselm – scion of a wealthy
merchant family, confidant of the dukes
of Burgundy and a counsellor of the

King of Scotland – had this chapel built in the likeness of the Church of the Holy
Sepulchre in Jerusalem, with the intention that he should be buried here with
his spouse. However, Anselm was killed and buried in Scotland. Only his heart
was later added to the tomb in Bruges. The decorative tombstone depicts
Anselm and Maragretha 'en gisant': lying stretched out with their heads on a
cushion and their hands folded in prayer. Anselm is dressed as a knight, with a
lion at this feet, symbolizing courage and strength. Margaretha is dressed as a
noblewoman; at her feet rests a dog, symbolizing faithfulness.

## ▤ MUSEUM SHOP

'Whoever enters the museum shop of
the Groeninge Museum will leave with
some wonderful memories, that I can
assure you. Perhaps you will take home
your favourite art treasures in the
shape of a handsomely illustrated book
or a reproduction on a poster maybe, or

depicted on a few picture postcards. And why don't you surprise yourself with an
original souvenir? I have caught not only some of my delighted fellow curators buying just such a present for themselves, but my wife as well!'

der why people from all corners of the
world have always found the Flemish
primitives so absorbing. The answer
perhaps lies in the fact that for the very
first time in art history we are confront-
ed with recognisable people and familiar
objects that correspond to today's reality. Even a Madonna seems to look like
the woman from around the corner. The
Flemish primitives laid the foundation of
an artistic concept that in its realism is
perfectly recognisable and therefore un-
derstandable to a modern-day observer.
The Flemish primitives discovered the

individual. Quite a feat. Those Flemish
painters were also dab hands at solving
the problems. They explored space in an
incredibly skilful and sophisticated way,
for example by placing a mirror somewhere in the room. In Memling's diptych,
a round mirror on the left-hand side behind the Madonna reflects the interior
she is sitting in. In it, her own silhouette
is painted just a whisker away from the
silhouette of the patrician Maarten van
Nieuwenhove, Memling's patron. Truly
magnificent. Are these works of art still
capable of moving me?

Absolutely. For pure emotion a painter
like Rogier van der Weyden touches me
more deeply than Jan van Eyck. The
works of van Eyck or Memling impress
me more with their intellectual and
conceptual qualities. Van der Weyden
and van Eyck: it is worth visiting the
treasure houses of Bruges, even if only
for the pleasure of enjoying these two
opposite ends of artistic spectrum.'

# Till-Holger Borchert
## Best addresses

## FAVOURITE SPOT

» **The churches of Bruges**

'The great churches of Bruges possess wonderful art collections, containing pieces that wouldn't disgrace any top-flight museum. Don't forget to look up at the tower of the Church of Our Lady. It is, with its 115,5 metres, the second tallest brick church-building in the world. When in Saint Saviour's, do go and marvel at the frescoes in the baptistery. And Saint James' Church is worth its while for the impressive **mausoleum of the De Gros family**, because this sculptural masterpiece reveals par excellence the self-confidence and power of the Burgundian elite.'

## RESTAURANTS

» **Den Amand**, Sint-Amandsstraat 4, tel. +32 (0)50 34 01 22, www.denamand.be, closed on Wednesday and Sunday

'In Den Amand I once saw a German restaurant critic copy out the entire menu card. You can't get higher praise than that! A small and elegant bistro, where you will find both tourists and local people enjoying the excellent food.'

» **Rock Fort**, Langestraat 15, tel. +32 (0)50 33 41 13, www.rock-fort.be, closed on Saturday and Sunday

'Rock Fort serves original, contemporary dishes with a modern twist. It's cooking is so good that the place is packed all week long. Local people love it, and I also like to pop in from time to time. But be careful: it is closed during the weekends.'

» **'t Schrijverke**, Gruuthusestraat 4, tel. +32 (0)50 33 29 08,
www.tschrijverke.be, closed on Monday

'This homely restaurant is named after a poem by Guido Gezelle, which hangs in a place of honour next to the door. But 't Schrijverke is above all rightly famed for its delicious regional dishes and its "Karmeliet" beer on tap.'

» **Tanuki**, Oude Gentweg 1, tel. +32 (0)50 34 75 12, www.tanuki.be,
closed on Monday and Tuesday

'A true temple of food, where you immediately drop your voice to the level of a whisper, so that you don't disturb the silent enjoyment of the other diners. In the open kitchen the chef does magical things with sushi and sashimi, and prepares his seven course menus with true oriental serenity.'

» **Den Gouden Harynck**, Groeninge 25, tel. +32 (0)50 33 76 37, www.dengouden
harynck.be, closed on Saturday (until 7.00 p.m.), Sunday and Monday and
most public holidays

'Den Gouden Harynck is a household name in Bruges, known and loved by foodies of all kinds. It is also one of the most pleasant star-rated restaurants in the city – as anyone who has ever been there will tell you.'

## CAFÉS

» **Delaney's Irish Pub & Restaurant**,
Burg 8, tel. +32 (0)50 34 91 45,
www.delaneys.be, no closing day,
but closed every morning (until
12.00 noon) and also in the afternoon
from Monday to Friday (between
3.00 p.m. and 6.00 p.m.)

'It's always party time in this Irish pub, with its distinctive international atmosphere. Delaney's is the kind of place where you can rub shoulders with the whole world at the bar.'

» **The Druid's Cellar**, Sint-Amandsstraat 11, tel. +32 (0)50 61 41 44, www.
thedruidscellar.eu, no closing day, but closed every morning (until 11.00 a.m.)

'I like to drop in at The Druid's Cellar every now and again, even if only to watch Drew, my favourite barkeeper, in action. Or simply to relax and enjoy a glass from their wide range of Scottish and Irish whiskies. They always taste just that little bit better in The Druids.'

» **Café Marcel**, Niklaas Desparsstraat 7-9, tel. +32 (0)50 33 55 02,
www.hotelmarcel.be, no closing day

'You can find this brand new café right in the heart of the city centre. Café Marcel is Bruges' refined version of a contemporary vintage café. In other words, a café from the days of yesteryear, but in a tight, new design setting. Think of dark wooden floorboards, simple lamps, leather benches and original wood panelling. You can pop in here for a tasty breakfast or an aperitif with tapas. A welcome new discovery!'

» **Den Express**, Stationsplein, tel. +32 (0)50 38 88 85,
www.horeca-station-brugge.be, no closing day

'The Den Express station bar is ideal for people like me, who travel a lot. Here I can enjoy a quiet coffee before setting off on my journey, safe from all the hustle and bustle going on outside.'

» **Hollandse Vismijn**, Vismarkt 4, tel. +32 (0)50 33 33 01, closed on Tuesday

'Whenever I fancy one of the popular Belgian beers, you will probably find me in the Hollandse Vismijn. This cheap and cheerful 'people's pub' is on the Fish Market. It is the type of café where everybody knows everybody and where you always get a warm welcome. Cheers!'

## SHOPPING LIST

» **Antiquariaat Van de Wiele**, Sint-Salvatorskerkhof 7, tel. +32 (0)50 33 63 17,
www.marcvandewiele.com, closed on Tuesday, Wednesday and Sunday

'For art and history I was fortunate enough to discover Marc Van de Wiele Antiques. This is undoubtedly one of the best addresses in a city that is rich in antique shops. The place to find unique, illustrated books from days long gone by.'

» **Boekhandel De Reyghere**, Markt 12, tel. +32 (0)50 33 34 03,
www.dereyghere.be, closed on Sunday

'For all my other reading material I rely on De Reyghere, located on the Market Square. Foreign visitors feel instantly at home in this book and newspaper store, primarily because of the large number of international titles it has on sale.'

» **Den Gouden Karpel**, Vismarkt 9-10-11, tel. +32 (0)50 33 33 89,
www.dengoudenkarpel.be, closed on Sunday and Monday

'The fishing family Ameloot have been running Den Gouden Karpel with heart and soul for many years. It is not only an excellent fish shop with an equally excellent catering service, but is also a really great fish bar. If you don't want the bother of making your own fish dish at home, in the bar you can sample oysters (European or Japanese), winkles, whelks, Zeebrugge fish soup, crab claws, half lobsters, fresh-salmon quiche, shrimp croquettes, etc. For a fish-lover like myself, it is hard to walk past Den Gouden Karpel without stopping to buy something.'

» **D's Deldycke Traiteurs**, Wollestraat 23, tel. +32 (0)50 33 43 35,
www.deldycke.be, closed on Tuesday

'In the 15$^{th}$ century the Spaniard Pedro Tafur was already praising Bruges for its wide available selection of exotic fruits and rare spices. The Deldycke caterer is proud to continue this centuries-old tradition. Here, all your culinary wishes will be fulfilled.'

» **Parallax**, Zuidzandstraat 17, tel. +32 (0)50 33 23 02, www.parallax.be,
closed on Sunday morning (in January, February, July and August:
whole Sunday) and public holidays

'I always buy my socks at Parallax, but they are also experts at stylishly camou-flaging my beer belly! Highly recommended for other fashion victims and the ves-timentally challenged! Boss, Scabal, Zilton, Falke: you can find them all here.'

---

## SECRET TIP

» **Museumshop**, Arentshof, Dijver 16,
www.museabrugge.be,
closed on Monday

» **Gezelle Museum, Jerusalem
Chapel and Lace Centre, Our Lady
of the Pottery** and **Folklore Museum**:
info on pages 80, 83, 85 and 90

'Whenever I want to take a breather, I saunter down Saint Anne's, Bruges' most striking working-class neighbourhood. You can still sense the charm of an authen-tic community in the streets around the Folklore Museum. The area boasts many fascinating places, too. Off the cuff, if I may: Our Lady of the Pottery, the Lace Centre, medieval **Jerusalem Chapel** and the Gezelle Museum.'

# The art of bobbins and pins

## Kumiko Nakazaki hopes
## to gain immortality through lace

It is now over a quarter-century since Kumiko Nakazaki from Japan
set foot in Bruges for the very first time. In the meantime, she has
blossomed into a true lace expert, who understands like no one else
how important lace is for Bruges.

**IDENTIKIT**

**Name:** Kumiko Nakazaki
**Nationality:** Japanese
**Date of birth:** 8 January 1956
Has lived in Bruges part-time since 1989.
Kumiko is affiliated to the Lace Centre
and publishes books about lace.

At university, Kumiko Nakazaki specialised in French literature, more specifi-
cally the 19<sup>th</sup> century symbolic poets.
But she felt nothing for an academic career. That is why she decided to go on
vacation for a year; to try and figure out
what direction she wanted to take with
her life. It was in the middle of this 'career crisis' that she by chance attended
a Belgian exhibition about ... lace.
'I learned that lace can grow very old,
can survive a very long time, and decided that I wanted to do something that
would live on for many years after my
death.' Straight away, Kumiko booked a
tour through Belgium, stopped for a day
in Bruges and ended up at the Lace
Centre, where she immediately made
clear that she would love to learn more
about lace-making. 'I returned to Japan
with the idea of living in Bruges and immediately applied for a student visa.'
At first, Kumiko found the change of
continents very difficult. 'During the

first years, you focus on the differences,
but after a while you start to notice simi-
larities.' As a result, she extended her
visa nine times! After almost a decade,
she had mastered the intricacies of
lace-making and designing. She had
even published a number of books about

*'As long as skilled and passionate people want
to make lace and are prepared to continually learn,
Bruges will remain the world's undisputed lace capital.'*

lace. In other words, she had accomplished more than enough to leave Bruges, but she couldn't bring herself to do it. 'Bruges has become my second home, a part of my life. I now have many friends here. And so for years I have been shuttling back and forth between my Japanese home and Bruges. Sometimes I work in Japan, sometimes in Bruges. Both places give me everything I need: I can start working straight away in either of them, without losing any time. In fact, I do just the same things in Bruges as I do in Japan: drawing, drawing and more drawing. There is not much time left over to do anything else.'

## LACE THROUGH THE CENTURIES

The history of lace in Belgium has its origins in the 16th century. It is generally assumed that bobbin lace was invented in Flanders, while needle lace probably originated in Venice. Whatever the truth of the matter, lace production became artistically, economically and socially important in Bruges in the years around 1550. The trade was protected and lace education was regulated. The religious orders (in particular, the nuns of Our Lady of Assumption and Our Lady of the Immaculate Conception) played a key role training poor girls to master the lace trade in special lace schools, where they also received a decent general education. In 1847, there were no fewer than 87 lace schools active in Bruges.

From 1850 onwards, lace-making evolved into a cottage industry. During the second half of the 19th century there were about 10,000 domestic lace-makers at work. This was exploitation of a massive scale; the lace merchants paid the women less than half of the average wage at the time. However, after the First World War the demand for hand-made lace fell dramatically and today lace-making is virtually non-existent as an economic activity. Fortunately, the people of Bruges managed to keep the old skills alive and have passed on this knowledge from generation to generation. Did you know that a simple method to learn lace-making was developed in the Bruges Lace College (founded in 1911) and that this method is now used all over the world? The lace techniques are taught by means of different colours: simple and the same in any language! Nowadays, various training courses are still organised in the Bruges Lace Centre, revealing the tricks of the lace trade to an increasing number of enthusiasts from every corner of the world.

*And why not visit the permanent exhibition in the Lace Museum of the renovated Lace Centre, located at Balstraat 16. (more information on the Lace Centre is available on pages 83-84 and on www.kantcentrum.eu)*

## Straddling the past and the future

'Whenever I shuttle between Belgium and Japan, I always ask myself over and over why I ever left in the first place. I love Bruges, because the city radiates enormous grandeur but is also is easy to come to terms with. You can cross it by foot in less than an hour. Bruges is a city on a human scale – which is pure luxury for me. I also love New York and Tokyo, but only as a tourist. In those huge cities, everything is so much bigger and faster; they are also too modern for me. Bruges cherishes its past and its age-old lace tradition is an inextricably part of the city. Here, lace is not merely something you find in a museum or buy in a specialised shop; in Bruges, lace is part of daily life. Virtually every inhabitant of Bruges has lace somewhere in his house. I am convinced that there are still many lace treasures hidden in Bruges attics.'
In order to survive, the lace industry in Bruges must be more than just a fine tradition. 'You have to strike the right balance. We need to respect the authentic traditions and the old techniques, but this is not enough; we must also dare to innovate and to give a more important place to creativity. With an open mind, without imposing any restrictions on ourselves, we must move forward towards the lace of tomorrow. The contemporary lace industry is standing with one foot in the past and one foot in the future.'

This is not always an easy position to be in – but Kumiko has managed it for decades. The Japanese lace expert successfully unites the two worlds: 'During my early years in Belgium, lace-making was a huge secret. It was an art that belonged to the city and was not to be shared. I was the first "foreigner", for whom the lace door was opened. Since then, many dozens of lace enthusiasts from all over the world have followed lace courses in Bruges. And as long as skilled and passionate people want to make lace and are prepared to continually learn, Bruges will remain the world's undisputed lace capital.'

# Kumiko Nakazaki
## Best addresses

### FAVORITE SPOT

» **Prinselijk Begijnhof Ten Wijngaarde (Beguinage)**, tel. +32 (0)50 33 00 11, www.monasteria.org

'Obviously I am not the only one who loves the **Beguinage**, with its white-painted houses and sober garden. It is a serene oasis in the middle of the city, a place in which you can find peace and contentment.'

### RESTAURANTS

» **'t Oud Handbogenhof**, Baliestraat 6, tel. +32 (0)50 33 71 18, www.hotel depauw.be, closed during the day (until 6.00 p.m., on Sunday until 12.00 p.m.), closed on Wednesday and Thursday

'People have been eating at this site since the 15th century. And nothing much has changed. It is still the same atmospheric restaurant, where you can enjoy typical local cooking and seasonal dishes.'

» **Poules Moules**, Simon Stevinplein 9, tel. +32 (0)50 34 61 19, www.poules moules.be, closed on Monday (except in July, August and December)

'I only recently discovered this place: it is the address in Bruges for mussels, which is the specialty of the house. And if the weather permits, you can sit on the delightful terrace with its view of the Simon Stevinplein.'

» **Sint-Barbe**, Sint-Annaplein 29, tel. +32 (0)50 33 09 99, www.sintbarbe.be, closed on Tuesday and Wednesday

'This cosy restaurant, where you can order home-made shrimp croquettes, steak or veal kidneys, is located in the shadow of the charming Saint Anna's Church.'

» **De Pepermolen**, Langestraat 16, tel. +32 (0)50 49 02 25, www.depepermolen.com, closed on Wednesday and Thursday

'In this restaurant in the always bubbling Langestraat you can enjoy one of their seasonal dishes or try their monthly discovery menu. King crab, carpaccio of beef, fresh soused herrings... Need I say more?'

» **De Middenstand**, 't Zand 20, tel. +32 (0)50 34 17 50, www.demiddenstand.com, closed on Wednesday

'It's great to sit on the terrace overlooking the square 't Zand and just watch the world go by. This address is famous for its fresh home-made dishes. The owner of the restaurant is also the chef – which is always a good sign!'

## CAFÉS AND TEAROOMS

» **Li O Lait**, Dweersstraat 30, tel. +32 (0)50 70 85 70, www.liolait.be, closed on Sunday and Monday

'A good breakfast, a filter coffee made grandma's way, a *mocha latte*, an ice coffee, a glass of cava, a bagel or a piece of cake... At any time of the day, you can enjoy yourself at Li O Lait.'

» **Tearoom Carpe Diem**, Wijngaardstraat 8, tel. +32 (0)50 33 54 47, www.tearoom-carpediem.be, closed on Tuesday

'Located in a fabulous 17th century building near the Beguinage, you can enjoy the delights of the Detavernier Bakery and its attractive adjoining tearoom, where you can choose from their great selection of home-made cakes and other delicacies. It's a place where I enjoy coming to relax.'

» **Café Vlissinghe**, Blekersstraat 2, tel. +32 (0)50 34 37 37, www.cafevlissinghe.be, closed on Monday and Tuesday

'This is one of the oldest pubs of the city. The beer has been flowing here since 1515 and the original medieval bar really takes you back in time. During the winter, it's great to gather around the warmth of the stove; during the summer, you can enjoy yourself on the outdoor terrace near the petanque court.'

» **De IJsbeer**, Noordzandstraat 73, tel. +32 (0)50 33 35 34. www.ijsbeerbrugge.be, closed on Sunday, except in July and August (depending on the weather and the events)

'I only eat ice cream when I am in De IJsbeer, which has been making traditional Italian ice cream here since 1922. You can taste the freshness of the ingredients. Normally, I just stick to a cone with a couple of scoops of ice cream, but occasionally I treat myself to one of their delicious ice cream cups.'

» **De Torre**, Langestraat 8, tel. +32 (0)50 34 29 46, www.de-torre.com, closed on Wednesday and Thursday, except in July, August and during the (Belgian) school holidays

'I like to drink a tea or coffee on the sunny terrace of De Torre, with its view of the Predikherenrei. And, having a sweet-tooth, I can almost never resist one of their delicious pancakes, waffles or a piece of apple pie.'

## SHOPPING ADDRESSES

» **'t Apostelientje**, Balstraat 11, tel. +32 (0)50 33 78 60, www.apostelientje.be, closed on Sunday afternoons, Monday and Tuesday morning (until 1.00 p.m.)

'For almost three decades, 't Apostelientje has been the place-to-be in Bruges for hand-made lace of the finest quality, offering an excellent choice of both contemporary and antique pieces. The service is both knowledgeable and helpful. True professionals at work!'

» **The Lace Centre Shop**, Balstraat 16, tel. +32 (0)50 33 00 72, www.kantcentrum.eu, no closing day

'Lace-lovers must visit the renovated Lace Centre, which is located in the old lace school once run by the Sisters of the Immaculate Conception. You can register to take part in a lace-making course and in the shop you can purchase beautiful pieces of lace and everything you need to make lace yourself.' *(Also see page 83)*

» **Ark van Zarren**, Zuidzandstraat 19, tel. +32 (0)50 33 77 28, www.arkvanzarren.be, closed on Sunday, except in December, during the (Belgian) school holidays and from the beginning of the Easter holidays until late August
'This is a great place to browse, right in the centre of town, where you can find different types of linen, fragrant soaps and special wallpapers. Romantic and rustic.'

» **Scharlaeken Handwerk**, Philipstockstraat 5, tel. +32 (0)50 33 34 55, www.scharlaeken.be, closed on Sunday, on public holidays and on Tuesday morning (until 1.45 p.m.)
'If you like lace-making or embroidering, you will find your way blindfold to this handiwork Walhalla. Scharlaeken Handwerk is specialised in lace-making, embroidery and knitting kits. There is also a fine selection of books, special linen, accessories and exclusive lace material.'

» **Rococo**, Wollestraat 9, tel. +32 (0)50 34 04 72, www.rococobrugge.be, no closing day
'As long ago as 1833 Rococo was acquiring fame and fortune thanks to its unique lace creations. Nowadays, it specializes in the sale of traditional handcrafted lace work, both past and present. This is the address in Bruges for anyone who wants to buy antique lace. The shop also gives regular lace demonstrations and their expert staff will answer all your lace questions with great professionalism.'

## SECRET TIP

» **Saint Saviour's Cathedral**, Steenstraat, tel. +32 (0)50 33 61 88, www.sintsalvator.be
'Now that the Saint Saviour's Cathedral has finally been freed from its renovation scaffolding, it shines like never before. On the beautifully laid-out cathedral square, you can share in the enjoyment of the children playing on the stone steps and the grassy lawns.'

# Focus on the Great War

Sharon Evans, in search
of the First World War

Just a handful of kilometres from Bruges lies the Westhoek region.
This green and pleasant land is now a haven of peace, but precisely
one hundred years ago, between 1914 and 1918, it was the setting for
some of the most terrible fighting the world has ever seen. It was
the Westhoek that first brought Sharon Evans to Belgium many years
ago. Nowadays, this Bruges 'settler' leads visitors on tours of the
old battlefields.

## IDENTIKIT

Name: Sharon Evans
Nationality: Australian
Date of birth: 9 September 1965
Has lived in Bruges since 1991. Sharon runs Quasimodo and organises bus trips to the Westhoek, where she gives guided tours to many hundreds of tourists.

Sharon was born in Asia, as the daughter of a serving Australian soldier. Having moved from place to place in that part of the world several times during her formative years, she eventually decided that the time had come to see what things were like on the other side of the planet! A year later, her wanderlust had still not been satisfied, and so she decided to 'hang around for a bit longer' in Europe. The choice was between Bruges and Vienna. 'I felt that Bruges was smaller, prettier, cleaner and friendlier – and so I chose Flanders.' Today, many years later, this citizen of the world still lives and works in Bruges. Her very first visit to Belgium – and the reason why she was so determined to come to our little country – took Sharon to the Westhoek. This was the place where her great-grandfather, together with his many comrades, had fought side by side during the Great

*'In the Westhoek I had the feeling that I was following in my great-grandfather's footsteps. Here in Flanders, I discovered a piece of my own history.'*

## 14-18: THE WAR IN IMAGES | BRUGES IN THE GREAT WAR

Bruges commemorates the Great War with three exhibitions at a single location. A historical section with photographs, posters, portraits and uniforms tells the story of Bruges during the war. The curator is Sophie De Schaepdrijver. In a second exhibition, Magnum photographer Carl De Keyzer shows a selection of original photographs illustrating aspects of the First World War, selected with a contemporary view in mind and with explanatory texts by David Van Reybrouck. In the third exhibition, ten other international Magnum photographers show their own work on the theme of war, reflecting on this sad subject in their own manner and from their own perspective. *Stadshallen (Belfort), until 22 February 2015 (See page 94)*

## BRUGES, OCCUPIED CITY

Less well-known – because the history of the Great War mainly focuses on places at the front – is the fact that during the First World War Bruges was the German headquarters for operations on the Atlantic coast. Shortly after the German Marine Infantry had installed their occupation regime in the city, the German High Command decided to convert the harbour at Zeebrugge into a base for their submarine fleet. Bruges also served as a place of relaxation for the German Army and – for the officers, at least – as a place of culture. After serving at the front for a period of 3 to 6 months, German soldiers were allowed a stay of 2 to 4 weeks in Bruges, to rest and recuperate.

If you want to see and experience for yourself the places where the Great War was fought one hundred years ago, you need to travel to the Westhoek. You can find a number of suggestions in the chapter 'Excursions from Bruges' (See page 155-158).

War. 'I am the daughter of a soldier, so I already knew quite a lot about the First World War. And I have always been interested in history; I guess it's just built into my genes! Besides, the Great War was very important for the Australian people. It's true that we lost many of our finest sons, but out of that suffering we discovered our identity as a nation.'

## The fascinating Westhoek

On her very first day in Belgium, Sharon immediately set off for the Westhoek. 'It's a wonderful place, with an undulating and easy-going landscape.' It was also an emotional place for Sharon. 'I had the feeling that I was following in my great-grandfather's footsteps. Walking where he had walked, remembering how he had struggled and fought here

all those years ago... It was a really moving and deeply personal experience. Here in Flanders, I discovered a piece of my own history. People who have never been here before find it hard to imagine that this delightful countryside was once a terrible battlefield, full of misery and death. In Tyne Cot Cemetery, the largest British military cemetery on the European mainland, there is a huge memorial wall engraved with the names of 35,000

### BRUGES AND THE GREAT WAR

In the course of 2015, there will be numerous events relating to the First World War on the Bruges cultural agenda. You can find more information and a full summary on www.brugge1418.be.

## THE RAID ON ZEEBRUGGE

Aanval van Zeebrugge — Engelsch torpedoboot « Iphigen » blokkeerende de haven. Attaque de Zeebrugge — Torpilleur anglais « Iphigen » bloquant le port Attack of Zeebrugge — English torpedo boat « Iphigen » blockading the port.

During the First World War, Zeebrugge – the outport of Bruges – was transformed into a highly sophisticated submarine base, with the intention of cutting off the overseas supply lines to England. As a result, the British decided to attack the harbour. On 23 April 1918, Saint George's Day, a flotilla under Vice-Admiral Keyes made an attempt to block the entrance to the harbour, so that the German U-boats could cause no further damage. This famous raid, one of the most high-risk operations during the entire war, is still commemorated each year.

soldiers who went 'missing', whose bodies were never found. 35,000! Something like that cannot fail to touch you. In the meantime, I have been back to the Westhoek thousands of times, but I will never forget that very first time. And no matter how often I come, it never ceases to make an impression. It's that kind of place; it gets under your skin...'

In 1991 Sharon founded the forerunner of Quasimodo. Originally, she offered her tourist customers both cycling and bus tours, but she eventually decided to concentrate on the latter. Today she runs Quasimodo with her husband, Philippe. The couple have two tours: *WWI Flanders Fields Tour* and *Triple Treat: the best of Belgium in one day*.
*(You can find more info on www. quasimodo.be and on pages 149 and 155)*

# Sharon Evans
## Best addresses

### FAVOURITE SPOT

**» The canals around Bruges**

'As soon as you leave the city, you find yourself in another world: a green paradise. Whoever follows the Bruges-Ghent Canal or the **Damse Vaart** (Damme Canal), exploring the region by bike, is treated to one picture-postcard scene after another. Not to be missed!'

### RESTAURANTS

**» Heer Halewijn**, Walplein 10, tel. +32 (0)50 33 92 61, closed on Monday, Tuesday and during the day (until 6.30 p.m.)

'Heer Halewijn shines brightly on the beautiful Walplein square, which is one of the city's less well-known jewels. You shouldn't expect any gastronomic hocus-pocus here, just good, honest grilled dishes, accompanied by a fine selection of top-quality wines.'

**» Taj Mahal**, Philipstockstraat 6, tel. +32 (0)487 14 74 86 and +32 (0)50 34 22 42, www.tajmahalrestaurant.be, closed on Monday

'I was born in Asia, so of course I like piquant Asian food. And fortunately you can find this in Bruges. I like to order my Indian curries from the Taj Mahal. Hot and spicy!'

**» Narai Thai**, Smedenstraat 43, tel. +32 (0)50 68 02 56, www.naraithai.be, no closing day

'The Narai Thai is another culinary hot-spot: both literally and figuratively! Here you can enjoy dishes ranging from the mildly spicy to punishingly peppery, and all set in a trendy lounge atmosphere. It's almost like being transported to the other side of the world, even if only for an hour or so.'

» **De Vlaamsche Pot**, Helmstraat 3-5, tel. +32 (0)50 34 00 86, www.devlaamschepot.be, closed on Monday and Tuesday
'Eccentric, yet at the same time very traditionally Flemish. This sounds like a contradiction but the Vlaamsche Pot somehow manages to blend these two extremes together. In this somewhat unusual setting you can enjoy fish stew (*waterzooi*), meat stew (*karbonaden*) and mussels with chips. In other words, the better Flemish classics.'

» **In 't Nieuw Museum**, Hooistraat 42, tel. +32 (0)50 33 12 80, www.nieuw-museum.com, closed on Wednesday, Thursday and during the day (until 6.00 p.m.), except on Sunday at noon
'Carnivores will just love in 't Nieuw Museum, where delicious hunks of meat are cooked over a charcoal grill. From spare ribs to best end of neck to prime steak. And all in a delightfully relaxed atmosphere. Perfect for families.'

## CAFÉS

» **Lokkedize**, Korte Vulderstraat 33, tel. +32 (0)50 33 44 50, www. lokkedize.be, closed on Monday, Tuesday and during the day (until 6.00 p.m.)

'One of my very favourite places. A pleasant bar where you can always enjoy some rhythm & blues, a bit of rock 'n roll or a classic chanson. There are regular live performances and the kitchen stays open really late.'

» **Bistro Zwart Huis**, Kuipersstraat 23, tel. +32 (0)50 69 11 40, www.bistrozwarthuis.be, closed on Monday and Tuesday and every morning (until 11.30 a.m.)
'This protected monument was built in 1642 and the facade and the medieval bar-room are truly impressive. Since recently, you can enjoy a bite to eat, a glass of something pleasant and occasional live music.'

» **'t Stokershuis**, Langestraat 7, tel. +32 (0)50 33 55 88, www.stokershuis.com,
  closed on Tuesday and Wednesday and during the day (until 6.30 p.m.)
'Small is beautiful: that could easily be the motto of 't Stokershuis. A traditional city bar in mini-format, with bags of atmosphere. A place you'll find really hard to leave!'

» **Bistro Du Phare**, Sasplein 2, tel. +32 (0)50 34 35 90, www.duphare.be,
  no closing day, but closed every morning (until 11.30 a.m.)
'Bistro Du Phare is one of those increasingly rare addresses where you can nearly always find live music. A place to be savoured: great on the outside terrace (overlooking the water) in the summer, and cosy inside during the winter.'

» **Café Rose Red**, Cordoeaniersstraat 16, tel. +32 (0)50 33 90 51,
  www.caferosered.com, no closing day, but closed every morning
  (until 11.00 a.m.)
'This slightly out-of-the-way café is specialised in abbey beers and sells a good selection of the world's very best 'trappist' brews, which you can either drink in the pleasing interior or in the equally charming courtyard. And if you sample one trappist too many, you can always spend the night at the hotel next door, run by the same people!'

---

## SHOPPING LIST

» **Jofré**, Vlamingstraat 7, tel. +32 (0)50 33 39 60, www.jofre.eu,
  closed on Sunday
'Admittedly, this ladies clothing boutique is not the cheapest in town, but it has an excellent selection of timeless designs that are well worth the investment. The kind of shop that a woman could spend quite some time in!'

» **De Kaasbolle**, Smedenstraat 11, tel. +32 (0)50 33 71 54, www.dekaasbolle.be,
  closed on Wednesday and Sunday
'Whoever likes a delicious piece of beautifully matured cheese should definitely make their way to De Kaasbolle. From creamy Lucullus, the house cheese, through Tartarin Cognac (a fresh cow's milk cheese with Turkish raisins, marinated in French brandy) to the authentic Greek feta marinade: every one is a real treat for your taste buds.'

» **Da Vinci**, Geldmuntstraat 34, tel. +32 (0)50 33 36 50, www.davinci-brugge.be, open from 14/2 to 31/10, no closing day

'Whether it is freezing cold or tropically warm, there are always tourists and local people patiently queuing up outside this deservedly well-known ice-cream parlour. The number of different flavours is almost limitless, and everything – from the ice-cream itself to the sauces – is made on the premises.'

» **Chocolatier Dumon**, Eiermarkt 6, Walstraat 6 and Simon Stevinplein 11, tel. +32 (0)50 22 16 22, www.chocolatierdumon.be, the shop on the Eiermarkt is closed on Tuesday; the other shops have no closing day

'I have been a big fan of Dumon's traditionally-made, top-quality chocolate for years. The Bruges story of confectioner Stephan Dumon began in 1996 on the Eiermarkt. In the meantime, he has also opened a sales point in the Walstraat and an imposing shop on the Simon Stevinplein. But I remain faithful to his small and welcoming shop on the Eiermarkt, where the old saying "good things come in small packages" really applies!'

» **ShoeRecrafting**, Langestraat 13, tel. +32 (0)50 33 81 01, www.shoerecrafting.be, closed on Sunday and Monday

'Luc Decuyper learnt the cobbler's art at Delvaux and other famous names in the leather trade, and is the man I can always rely on when my shoes start showing signs of wear. This excellent craftsman obviously loves his work – and it really shows in the end result.'

## SECRET TIP

» **City Theatre**, Vlamingstraat 29, tel. +32 (0)50 44 30 60, www.ccbrugge.be

'For me, taking in a concert at the City Theatre (Stadschouwburg) is a real treat. Bruges **Royal City Theatre**, in the very heart of the old city, dates from 1869 and is an architectural masterpiece. Every time I visit, I never fail to enjoy the waves of red and gold in the palatial auditorium and the opulent splendour of the majestic foyer. Little wonder that the Bruges theatre is regarded as one of the best preserved city theatres in all Europe.'

Lissewege

# Excursions from **Bruges**

# The other Flemish art cities

## Antwerp (Antwerpen)   82 km

It is hard to describe Antwerp in a single word. This historic city has so much to offer: a beautiful cathedral and numerous imposing churches, a magnificent Central Station, the ground-breaking Museum on the River (MAS), the tranquil Rubens House, a delightful sculpture garden (Middelheim), a unique zoo and so much more. Antwerp is also Belgium's fashion capital, home to many internationally renowned designers. That is why in the Scheldt city you will find dozens of exclusive boutiques, rubbing shoulders with fun bric-a-brac shops where you can browse for hours: it's every fashionista's dream! Not surprisingly, the local 'Antwerpenaars' – who are fairly loud by nature – are extremely proud of their city. Welcome to Antwerp, the most self-confident city in Belgium.

**INFO >** www.antwerpen.be; there is a direct train connection between Bruges and Antwerp (journey time: 1 hour and 28 minutes; www.belgianrail.be)

## Brussels (Brussel)   88 km

The whole world comes together in Brussels, with a different continent around every corner. It is a city bursting with life, from the exotic Matonge quarter to the stately elegance of the European institutions. The capital of Belgium has a vibrancy like no other and the formality of its 'hard' metropolitan structure is softened by the authentic, working-class ambiance of its more popular districts. On his platform not far from the majestic Market Square, *Manneke Pis* – the unfortunate symbol of Belgium – is permanently peeing. And this diverse city even knows how to rec-

oncile the chic sophistication of the Zavel with the folksy informality of the Vossenplein. Royalty watchers rush eagerly to the Paleizenplein, art fans indulge themselves in the Magritte Museum, the Royal Museums or the Horta Museum, foodies hurry to the numerous food temples, and vintage-lovers climb to the top of the Atomium. In short, Brussels has something for everyone. **INFO >** www.brussel.be, www.visitbrussels.be; there is a direct train connection between Bruges and Brussels Central Station (journey time: 1 hour and 2 minutes; www.belgianrail.be)

## Ghent (Gent)   39 km

No other people are as stubborn and as self-willed as the people of Ghent – or the Gentenaars, as they are known. It is built into their genes. In the Middle Ages, the Gentenaars revolted against the Count of Flanders and later they formed the first trade union, but they also built many great monuments and churches. You can admire the magnificent *Lamb of God* altarpiece in Saint Bavo's Cathedral, before settling down on

one of the many terraces along the Graslei or Korenlei. Afterwards, you can take in the stately Belfry, the much-discussed new city hall and the less controversial old town hall (a splendid building with protected monument status). There is also the Gravensteen, a fortress built in 1180, and the nearby Patershol, a medieval neighbourhood full of crooked streets and winding alleyways. The House of Alijn, the Design Museum, the SMAK (Museum of Contemporary Art) and the STAM (City Museum) are all distinctive and thought-provoking. The same words could also be used to describe Ghent's large student population and the colourful vibe they create in the city's nightlife and cultural scene. The highlight of the year is the world famous 'Gentse Feesten' (Ghent Festival), an annual high mass of culture that sets the entire Artevelde city on fire! **INFO >** www.gent.be, www.visitgent.be; there is a direct train connection between Bruges and Gent-Sint-Pieters Station (journey time: 23 minutes; www.belgianrail.be)

## Louvain (Leuven)   110 km

Louvain is without a doubt the number one student city in Belgium. Dozens of historic university buildings are spread all over the old city centre. As a result, you come across students everywhere, moving from one campus to another. Leuven can proudly boast the largest and oldest university in Belgium, founded as long ago as 1425. Nowadays you

can visit many of the university colleges and the magnificent university library. Alternatively, you can admire the remarkable Cloth Hall and the imposing Market Square, or spend a fascinating few hours in Museum M. And if you want to sample the carefree ambiance of student life, why not head down to the Oude Markt (Old Market), which is perhaps the longest bar in the world...

**INFO >**www.visitleuven.be; there is a direct train connection between Bruges and Leuven (journey time: 1hour and 28 minutes; www.belgianrail.be)

## Malines (Mechelen)   90 km

Although the smallest of the Flemish art cities, Mechelen is well worth a visit. Situated halfway between Antwerp and Brussels, Mechelen is more compact than these major players, but still has its fair share of wonderful historic buildings and heritage sites. The River Dijle meanders through the city, enclosed by the Zoutwerf (Salt Quay) with its 16th century wooden frontages and the Haverwerf (Oat Quay) with its pastel-coloured decorative facades. There is also the imposing Lamot brewery complex, which nowadays serves as a congress and heritage centre. Beautifully renovated in a daring and contemporary architectural style, it is a classic example of how upgrading industrial archaeology can bring new life to a city. But perhaps the most well-known sightseeing spot is the proud Saint Rombouts Cathedral; two carillons of bells hang in its 97metre-high tower and are often played by students of the Mechelen carillon school. Another 'must' is the former palace of Margaret of Austria. The Netherlands used to be governed from here, but nowadays it is a great place for a quiet stroll.

**INFO >** www.visitmechelen.be, www.uitinmechelen.be; from Bruges you can easily reach Mechelen by train (journey time 1 hour and 21 minutes, with one change at Gent-Sint-Pieters Station, www.belgianrail.be)

# The area around Bruges

## BRUGES' WOOD- AND WETLAND

The green area of wetlands and woodlands surrounding Bruges, known locally as the Ommeland, offers authentic villages, unspoiled countryside, beautiful castles and numerous cycling routes that lead through a landscape of endless beauty.

## ORGANIZED EXCURSION

### Triple Treat Quasimodo tour: The best of Belgium in one day

Take it easy on this English-language minibus tour, which takes you to, amongst others, the illustrious Tilleghem Castle and unique Neo-Gothic Loppem Castle. Included are a pleasant stroll through medieval Damme and a visit to the Gothic abbey barn of Ter Doest at Lissewege. And what would this tour be without some delicious waffles and mouth-watering chocolate. The tour ends with a visit to the Fort Lapin Brewery, just outside of Bruges.
**OPEN >** Excursions during the period 15/2 to 15/12: on Monday, Wednesday and Friday. You will be collected from your hotel or some other place of your choice in the city centre. Departure: 9.15 a.m.

Return: 5.15 p.m. Prior reservation is necessary.
**PRICE >** Including lunch and tickets: € 65.00; youngsters under 26: € 55.00; there is an immediate € 10.00 reduction when you also book the Quasimodo WWI Flanders Fields Tour *(More info on page 155)*
**INFO >** Tel. 0800 975 25 or +32 (0)50 37 04 70, www.quasimodo.be

## FREE EXCURSIONS

### Lissewege (Bruges)   10 km

It seems as if time has stood still in Lissewege. With its lovely little canal, white-painted polder houses and expansive fields, it serves as a model for the way every Flemish village used to be: charming, nostalgic and romantic. The

brick Church of Our Lady of Visitation is a textbook example of 'coastal Gothic'. Its remarkable interior has a miraculous statue of the Virigin Mary (1625), an exceptional organ case and a beautifully sculptured rood loft and pulpit (1652). Anyone who makes the effort to climb the 264 stairs of the truncated tower is rewarded with a panoramic view over the polders, stretching as far as Ostend and Bruges. On a clear day, you can even see Walcheren (Zeeland). Lissewege was already a place of pilgrimage in the Middle Ages. In a nearby creek, fishermen discovered the miraculous statue of the Virgin Mary and the church was built to house it. Pilgrims on the road to Santiago de Compostela stopped off in Lissewege and their gifts and donations helped to bring the village a certain prosperity. In 1106, French Benedictines were approached to found an abbey in Lissewege. Due to their neglect, the land on which the Thosan Chapel stood passed into the hands of the Cistercians and it was they who built the famous abbey complex of Ter Doest. Many farms were constructed in the (wide) area around the abbey, often on land that the monks had reclaimed from the sea. Sadly, of all the abbey buildings only the pigeon tower, the monumental gatehouse and the enormous 14th century abbey barn have withstood the ravages of time. You can read more about the 'white village' in the local visitors' centre that also houses a delightful Saints' Museum, with 120 antique statues of patron saints.

**INFO >** www.lissewege.be, www.visit-bruges.be or in the free inspiration guide *Zeebrugge-Lissewege-On-Sea* (issued by the City of Bruges). The train running between Bruges and Zeebrugge stops in Lissewege.

## Damme   6 km

The charming town of Damme, which was the transhipment port for the city of Bruges until the silting up of the formal tidal inlet Zwin, is located to the north-east of its larger neighbour. You can drive there along the straight line of the Damse Vaart (Damme Canal), which is lined with magnificent poplars. On sunny days, Damme seems like a giant terrace, but this small town has much more to offer than just excellent food and drink. Here you can 'meet' Jacob van Maerlant – one of the most important Middle Dutch authors – in front of the town hall and on the outskirts of town you can make the acquaintance of Tijl Uilenspiegel, the other hero of Damme. You can find out more about the pranks and jokes of this legendary rascal and about the cultural-historical context in which the

character came into being in the

🏛 Uilenspiegel Museum.

A fun way to travel between Bruges and
Damme is by water: the nostalgic 🏛
paddle steamer Lamme Goedzak –
named after the bosom friend of Tijl
Uilenspiegel – sails to and fro between
the Noorweegse (Norwegian) Quay in
Bruges and the mooring station in
Damme from the beginning of April to
the end of September. *(More info on
page 65)* Damme is also known as a book
town, with a large book market held
every second Sunday of the month.

**INFO >** www.toerismedamme.be and
www.bootdamme-brugge.be. Bus
no. 43 (not on Saturday, Sunday and
official holidays), stop: Damme Plaats
or via Sint-Kruis or Sijsele (bus no. 58);
by paddle steamer Lamme Goedzak
*(See page 65)*

## Loppem (Zedelgem)   6 km

Loppem is another village in the green
countryside around Bruges and contains
the beautiful Saint Martin's Church, the
Priory of Our Lady of Bethany, the old
Heidelberg toll-booth and, above all, the
neo-Gothic 🏛 Loppem Castle (a protected monument). This 19th century castle,
situated in the middle of a stunning English landscape garden and containing an
authentic maze, has played a prominent
role in Belgian history. In October 1918,
during the final liberation offensive of the
First World War, King Albert I moved his
headquarters to Loppem. A month later,
the so called 'Government of Loppem' –

the very first three-party alliance in Belgium – was formed here. Both the architecture and the original design of the castle are exceptionally well preserved and
the art collection is very impressive. Particularly noteworthy are the wall paintings with captions by the poet Guido
Gezelle. *(You can get to know more about
Guido Gezelle and his work in the Gezelle
Museum in Bruges, see page 80-81)*

**INFO >** www.kasteelvanloppem.be. Bus
no. 72, stop: Loppem Sportcentrum.

## Jabbeke   10 km

Jabbeke, the small town where the
Flemish expressionist painter-sculptor
Constant Permeke lived and worked for
more than twenty years, is located ten
kilometres south-west of Bruges. Permeke pursued his remarkable artistic
career in an equally remarkable villa,
The Four Winds, which was built to a
highly progressive design for its time,
commissioned by Permeke himself.
Nowadays, the villa houses the
🏛 Mu.ZEE Permeke Museum. You can
wander through the artist's former home
and garden, as well as visit his studio.

**INFO >** www.jabbeke.be and www.

take the time to stop at the historic lock complex of Plassendale (at the intersection of the Bruges-Ostend and Oudenburg-Nieuwpoort canals).
**INFO >** www.oudenburg.be and www.ram-oudenburg.be. Bus no. 54, stop: Oudenburg Plaats, or by train: Brugge-Oudenburg; from the train station, you take bus no. 21, 22 or 23

muzee.be. Bus no. 52 or no. 53, stop: Jabbeke Museum Permeke

## Oudenburg  16 km

Oudenburg is one of the oldest locations of human habitation in the Bruges region, with a settlement dating back to Roman times. It was here that the Romans constructed a 'castellum' to protect the coastal region from attacks from the sea. Tradition says that the Burg of Bruges was built with stones from the castellum of Oudenburg. In the Middle Ages, Oudenburg was able to prosper thanks to a thriving cloth industry. A milestone in the history of this small community was the foundation of the Saint Peter's Abbey in 1084 by Saint Arnold, who was then on a papal peace mission to Flanders. The old abbey site is now home to the ▣ Roman Archaeological Museum (Romeins Archeologisch Museum - RAM). Reconstructions, models, archaeological findings and computer simulations introduce you to the rich past of this fascinating town. A tip for cycling enthusiasts: Oudenburg is centrally located in the cycle network around Bruges. Make sure you

## Torhout  18 km

The most beautiful water castle in the vicinity of Bruges is located in Wijnendale, a village near Torhout. The ▣ Wijnendale Castle Museum will take you on a journey through 1,000 years of fascinating history by means of contemporary presentations and multimedia displays. You can see how Mary of Burgundy fell fatally from her horse nearby or watch as King Leopold III and the Belgian government part after the invasion of the Germans. Children can undertake a magical fairy-tale quest. The visitors' centre provides free information about Torhout, the Bruges 'Ommeland', regional products, hiking and cycling routes, etc. Pottery fans should pay a

visit to the 🏛 Museum Torhouts Aardewerk in the centre of Torhout. Unique pottery creations from the 16th to the 20th-century highlight the rich tradition of this almost lost artistic craft.

INFO > www.toerismetorhout.be, www.kasteelwijnendale.be. Train Bruges-Kortrijk; from the station in Torhout you take the bus no. 51 or no. 64, stop: Kasteel Wijnendale

## THE COAST

The Belgian coast is also close by. Catch a breath of fresh air on the wide sandy beaches and traffic-free promenades, enjoy the delicious delights of the many fish restaurants or take a look in one of the many interesting museums.

### Zeebrugge (Bruges)   14 km

Zeebrugge is more than just a world port. Anyone who looks beyond the remarkable skyline of the harbour will discover a wide, family-friendly beach, an exceptional nature reserve, a charming marina and a fishing port, where you can enjoy a contagious folksy ambiance and… shrimps with a beer! Thanks to this active fishing port, with its high-tech fish market and its many neighbouring fish restaurants, fish shops and fishermen pubs, you can have a great meal at any time of the day in the town they call 'the capital of fish'. A good way to explore the seaport of Bruges and its operations is to take a 🏛 harbour trip on the passenger boat 'Zephira'. The tour starts from the old fishing port and takes in the naval base, the Pierre Vandamme Lock (one of the largest locks in the world),

the gas terminal, the wind turbine park, the 'tern' island, the cruise ships and the dredging vessels. Each visitor is given an easy-to-use audio-visual guide in the desired language. You can also download the information on your smart phone. *(Read more about the harbour trip on page 86)* The 🏛 Seafront maritime theme park has been developed in the unique setting of the old fish market in Zeebrugge. Here you can discover the secrets of the sea, learn about the rich fishing history of the region and find out all you need to know about the bustling seaport of Bruges. Outside, you will visit the West-Hinder Lightship and descend into the hold of a genuine Russian submarine. *(Read more about Seafront Zeebrugge on page 86)*

From Zeebrugge you can easily join the bicycle network in the area around Bruges (Wood- and Wetland) or the coastal hiking and cycling routes that connect all the Flemish seaside resorts.

INFO > www.brugge.be/zeebrugge; www.franlis.be; www.seafront.be or the free inspiration guide *Zeebrugge – Lissewege-aan-Zee*. Train Bruges-Zee-

brugge, station: Zeebrugge-Dorp or Zeebrugge-Strand; to reach the port or seafront you can also take the coastal tram (direction: Knokke), stop: Zeebrugge-Kerk

## Ostend (Oostende)  22 km

Ostend is one of the most visited seaside resorts on the Belgian North Sea coast. As the favourite holiday resort of the Belgian royal house, the city boasts a rich royal past. At the beginning of the 20th century, King Leopold II spared neither expense nor trouble to make Ostend the 'Queen of Seaside Resorts', which in its time compared favourably with many of the foreign seaside resorts. The Casino, the Thermae Palace Hotel, the Royal Galleries, the wide promenade, the kiosk on the Wapenplein, the Leopold Park and the Wellington Racecourse all date from this period. Other eye-catchers in the 'City by the Sea' are: the Fishermans' Quay (Visserskaai), with the Icelandic trawler 'Amandine' and the unique Fish Staircase (Vistrap), the three-mast training vessel 'Mercator' (in the marina), the neo-Gothic Church of Saint Peter and Saint Paul (containing the tomb of Queen Louise-Marie), Fort Napoleon (on the east side of the harbour channel), the Raversyde domain - Prince Karel Memorial, the remains of the Atlantic Wall and the various other museums that are part of 🏛 Mu.ZEE Ostend. The former museum of fine art in the Romestraat houses a unique collection of Belgian art from 1830 to the present day, with works by James Ensor, Léon Spilliaert, Constant Permeke, Jean Brusselmans, Raoul De Keyzer, Roger Raveel, Panamarenko, Luc Tuymans and many others. This permanent display is one of the finest in all Flanders. In the 🏛 Ensor House near the Vlaanderenstraat, you can step into the fascinating world of Ostend's most famous painter. It was in this house – with the souvenir shop of his uncle and aunt on the ground floor – that James Ensor lived and worked. Sadly, you will no longer find original paintings by the great master here; these now hang in major museums all around the world. **INFO >** www.visitoostende.be; www.muzee.be. Train Bruges-Ostend

The Westhoek, fashioned from the fertile polders of Flanders, is a region of picturesque villages and historic cities, sandwiched between the French border and the North Sea coastal plain. It is a place that invites you to relax, but which is also closely associated with the tragic events of the First World War.

## ORGANIZED EXCURSIONS

*Various day trips are organized from Bruges to the Westhoek. Prior reservation is necessary.*

### Quasimodo WWI Flanders Fields Tour

A guide from Quasimodo takes you on a personal and memorable minibus trip to Passendale, Hill 60, Messines Ridge, the private museum at Hooge Crater in Zillebeke, several Commonwealth and German cemeteries, trenches and bunkers, the Menin Gate and numerous Australian, New Zealand, Canadian, British and Irish mon-

uments. In short, all the highlights! The stories told by the Quasimodo guides allow you to visualize the reality of four terrible years of war in the Ypres Salient. It is also possible to stay on in Ypres after the tour has ended, so that you can attend the Last Post ceremony at 8 p.m. In this case, you will be brought back to Bruges by taxi after the ceremony.

**LANGUAGE >** Explanation in English
**MEETING POINT >** You will be collected from your hotel or some other place of your choice in the city centre. Departure: 9.00 a.m. Return: 5.30 p.m.
**OPEN >** Excursions are conducted from Tuesday to Sunday in the period 1/2 to 31/12
**PRICE >** Including lunch and ticket Hooge Crater Museum: € 65.00; youngsters aged 8 to 25: € 55.00; there is an immediate € 10.00 reduction when you also book the Triple Treat Quasimodo tour: the best of Belgium in one day *(More info on page 149)*. People who opt to stay for the Last Post must pay the cost of the taxi ride separately.
**INFORMATION AND RESERVATIONS >** Tel. 0800 975 25 or +32 (0)50 37 04 70, www.quasimodo.be. Tickets are also available from the tourist offices on ⓘ 't Zand (Concertgebouw) and the Markt (Market Square - Historium)

## In Flanders Fields tour

This bus tour will take you to numerous sites of interest related to the war of 1914-1918. With expert guides, you will visit the *Grieving Parents* by Käthe Kollwitz in Vladslo, the trenches along the River IJzer, the John McCrae site at Essex Farm Cemetery near Boezinge and the mine craters at Hill 60. The trip also takes you to a number of remarkable war monuments: the Canadian *Brooding Soldier* (Sint-Juliaan), the French Guynemer monument (Poelkapelle) and the New Zealand Memorial in Passendale. The French military cemetery at Saint Charles de Potyze (just outside Ypres), the Belgian military cemetery at Houthulst and the world's largest Commonwealth military cemetery at Tyne Cot (near Passendale) are also included in the itinerary. The day is rounded off with a visit to the In Flanders Fields Museum in Ypres and the Last Post ceremony at the Menin Gate.

**LANGUAGE >** Explanation in English and German.

**MEETING POINT >** You are collected from your hotel at 10.00 a.m., departure from the bus stop at the Bargeplein/Kanaaleiland: 10.30 a.m. Return: 9.30 p.m.

**OPEN >** Every Thursday, Saturday and Sunday during the period 1/4 to 1/11 and also on 8/11 and 11/11

**PRICE >** Including lunch and ticket to the In Flanders Fields Museum: € 76.00; 65+ and students aged 12 to 26: € 69.00

## Flanders Fields Battlefield Daytours

Discover the most popular tourist attractions of the Westhoek and the Great War. You will visit the German cemetery at Langemark, Tyne Cot Cemetery in Passendale, the Memorial Museum Passchendaele 1917 in Zonnebeke, where you can enjoy a dug-out-tunnel experience, the Menin Gate, the City of Ypres with its magnificent Cloth Hall and the not-to-be-missed In Flanders Fields Museum. The tour continues to Hill 60, Hill 62 (craters and bunkers), Heuvelland and Kemmelbergl, Messines Ridge, the mine craters of 7 June 1917, trenches and various other war monuments.

**LANGUAGE >** Explanation in English, French and Dutch.

**MEETING POINT >** You are collected from your hotel. Departure: 8.45 a.m. Return: 5.15 p.m.

**OPEN >** Excursions from Tuesday to Sunday. No excursions during the period 13/1 to 31/1

**PRICE >** Including lunch, a local beer and a ticket to the In Flanders Fields Museum and the Memorial Museum Passchendaele 1917: € 70.00; students aged 18 to 26: € 67.00; youngsters aged 10 to 17: € 65.00

**ON REQUEST >** Tailor-made excursions (e.g. France). Short evening trip to the Last Post ceremony at the Menin Gate in Ypres. Departure: 6.15 p.m. Return: 9.15 p.m. Price: € 40.00

**INFORMATION AND RESERVATIONS >** Tel. 0800 99 133, www.visitbruges.org

## Great War Battlefields Tour

Make your acquaintance with all the most important places on the front of the First World War. With an experienced guide you will explore the Trench of Death in Diksmuide and other trench sites, such as Hill 60 in Zillebeke. The bus trip will also take you to the Canadian Memorial in Langemark-Poelkapelle, the impressive cemeteries in Boezinge, Tyne Cot Cemetery in Passendale and the Memorial Museum Passchendaele 1917 in Zonnebeke. In Ieper (Ypres) you will visit the In Flanders Fields Museum and can discover the rest of this historic front town at your own pace. You will end the day by attending the Last Post ceremony.

**LANGUAGE >** Explanation in English. Information available in Dutch and French.

**MEETING POINT >** Bargeplein (City map: E13), under the red awning. Departure: 9.00 a.m. Return: 9.15 p.m.

**OPEN >** During the period 28/3 to 29/12: every Tuesday, Thursday and Saturday. During the period 1/1 to 27/3 only on request. There will be no excursion on 31/12

**PRICE >** Including lunch (no drinks) and tickets to the In Flanders Fields Museum and the Memorial Museum Passchendaele 1917: € 79.00; children aged 6 to 12: € 39.00

**INFORMATION AND RESERVATIONS >** Tel. +32 (0)800 14 180, www.greatwar-battlefieldstour.com, www.tickets-brugge.be. Tickets are also available from the tourist offices ℹ on 't Zand (Concertgebouw) and the Markt (Market Square - Historium)

## WORLD WAR I REVISITED

In the course of 2015, there will be numerous events relating to the First World War in and around Bruges. You can find more information and a full summary on www.brugge1418.be

# FREE EXCURSIONS

## Ypres (Ieper)   46 km

Thanks to its flourishing cloth industry, Ypres, along with Bruges and Ghent, was one of the richest and most powerful cities in Flanders in the 13th century. Its strategically important position meant that Ypres was besieged on several occasions, which led to the construction of strong defensive ramparts around the city. The original medieval ramparts were significantly strengthened and extended by Vauban in the 17th century. Ypres continued to play a key strategic role during the First World War and was the scene of fierce fighting in the notorious the Ypres Salient. By the end of the war, the city was in ruins. It was rebuilt in a Neo-Gothic style, but the most important buildings are almost exact copies of the original buildings that had been destroyed. Saint Martin's Cathedral and the majestic Cloth Hall (with its 125 metre facade) were reconstructed in their 13th-14th century style, while the Lille Gate (Rijselsepoort) was restored in its 'Vauban' style. Visitors who wish to experience the impact that the First World War had on Ieper should definitely not miss the fascinating and interactive 🎧 In Flanders Fields Museum. You are given a poppy armband that automatically uploads your chosen language for the different museum displays, which tell the story of the horror of the trenches and the bombardment of the city through the lives of four real people.

**INFO >** www.toerismeieper.be; www.inflandersfields.be; there is a direct train connection with Ypres; from the station bus no. 1 or no. 95 will take you to the main market square (Ieper Markt)

# THE MEETJESLAND

## Adegem   19 km

The flat Flemish polder region, which is better known as 'Meetjesland' (literally meaning 'creek country'), is situated to the east of Bruges. The northern part of Meetjesland is characterised by water meadows and a series of ancient salt creeks; the southern part is more green and wooded. The central town of Eeklo, with the medieval Huysmans farm with the Regional Centre (Streekcentrum), the remarkable art-nouveau villa 'Aurora' and the unique 'Het Leen' arboretum, is well worth a visit. So too is the 🎧 Canada-Poland War Museum in the neighbouring town of Adegem. This double museum is the perfect place for anyone who wants to know what happened in Flanders during the Second World War. In the Canada War Museum, a number of lifelike tableaus reconstruct scenes from the front, including the Battle of the Leopold Canal (Battle of the Scheldt). There is also an excellent collection of pictures, weapons, radio transmitters and uniforms. For children there is the 'Second World War in miniature' in the Poland War Museum, where they can view the war's major battles on a scale of 1:35, special adjusted to the requirements of children. In both muse-

ums, the kids can take part in a fascinating photo search. And to recover from the misery of war, afterwards you can take a peaceful (guided) stroll in museum's themed gardens.

INFO > www.toerismemeetjesland.be; www.canadapolandmuseum.be. Bus no. 58 or no. 58S to Adegem; to reach the Canada-Poland War Museum: from the centre of Adegem, use the bell-bus service no. 185, stop Canadian Museum (please note: to make the necessary arrangements with the bell-bus, you need to telephone at least two hours in advance)

## THE FLEMISH ARDENNES

### Audenarde (Oudenaarde) 49 km

The region of green hills in the southern part of East Flanders, famous for its beautiful panoramic views, authentic villages, rolling fields, winding country paths and lovely rivers, is known as the 'Flemish Ardennes'. At the heart of the Flemish Ardennes lies the old town of Audenarde, mirrored in the tranquil waters of the River Scheldt. As well as the beautiful late-Gothic town hall with its MOU-museum and the imposing Baroque Saint Walburga's Church, the 🏛 'Tour of Flanders' multimedia centre is not to be missed. This centre, devoted to Flanders' most famous cycle race, contains an interactive 'perception' museum, an exhibition hall, a film auditorium,

a fun shop and – last but not least – the bike-friendly 'Flandrien' brasserie. In the museum, you can follow the virtual route of the race and thanks to the different multimedia techniques you can even become a key player in the finale of 'Flanders' Finest'. The info desk will tell you everything you need to know about sites of interest and the cycling infrastructure of the Flemish Ardennes. Tired cycling enthusiasts are even able to shower here!

INFO > www.toerismevlaamse ardennen.be; www.oudenaarde.be; www.crvv.be. Train Bruges-Oudenaarde; from the station in Audenarde take bus no. 17, 47 or 62, stop: Oudenaarde Markt.

# Index of street names